Abbey's Story

Sarah Boone

26 25 24 23 22   8 7 6 5 4 3 2 1

ABBEY'S STORY

Copyright ©2022 Sarah Boone

All Scripture taken from Holy Bible, New Living Translation, copyright © 1996, 2004, 2015 by Tyndale House Foundation. Used by permission of Tyndale House Publishers, Inc., Carol Stream, Illinois 60188. All rights reserved.

All Rights Reserved. Except as permitted under the U.S. Copyright Act of 1976, no part of this publication may be reproduced, distributed, or transmitted in any form by any means, or stored in a database or retrieval system, without the prior written permission of the author and/or publisher.

Published by:

Barefoot Publishing

www.publishbarefoot.com

Printed in the United States

CONTENTS

Preface		ix
1	Vacation	1
2	Home	11
3	The Accident	16
4	She Speaks	22
5	Ezekiel 16:6	28
6	Discharged	34
7	All Better Boo Boos	39
8	Walking with Jesus	47
9	Two Crosses	54
10	Flip Flops	61
11	Bonnie Jean	69
12	The Faith of a Child …	75
13	Bye Bye, Abbey	81

Dedication

To my wonderful husband, thank you for praying for me every time I would sit down to write and for pushing me outside of my comfort zone to do hard things I never thought I could do. I love you!

To my parents who were my intercessors every time I sat down to write and for reminding me of Who called me to do this! Thank you!

To my beautiful Abbey Joy who this story is written about. Your joy has and will always be a light in our lives. You truly carry the countenance of Heaven sweetheart!

To our other beautiful daughters, Hannah, Elizabeth and Faith and our son, Liam. Thank you for praying and for being a constant voice in my ears telling me to keep writing when I felt I wasn't worthy to tell such a precious story…and for helping with Liam so I could write! Liam, you are my other miracle and I am smitten by you my little love.

Finally, thank you to all our friends and family who cheered me on and prayed continuously for this to happen! Your love and faith for our family has meant the world to us.

Dedication

Preface

There are times in the lives of most people where they are faced with a challenge to do something that pulls them well outside of their comfort zone. Writing this book was one of these moments for me! Inside of the pages of this book, you are going to get an honest, heartfelt account of a miraculous testimony that took my family and me on a journey of faith, fear and finding a new strength in Jesus that we had never known.

I had asked my husband Jason to write this book on many occasions ever since our daughter's accident. When he would sit, pray, and pull out his laptop and attempt to start…the words and thoughts just didn't flow. Finally, one evening as he sat and attempted to begin the first chapter again, the Lord spoke to him and said, "This is not your story to write. I want Sarah to write it from her heart, from a mother's heart." That is what the following chapters are full of raw, real facts, fears and faith from a mama's heart doing her best to share a precious testimony that was born out of one of the scariest and heart wrenching moments of my life.

I have taken great care to share with you every fact, detail and recollection of Abigail's testimony. As a follower of Jesus and as the wife of a church planter, the current senior pastors of a church and as a Bible college graduate I wanted to be so very careful that this testimony held true to a few key principles that are important to me.

First, it had to line up with the truth of God's word, the Bible. I have been careful to submit my daughter's testimony to trusted pastors, leaders and people in our lives to ensure that the entire account doesn't contradict the truth of Scripture. Secondly, it is important to my family and I that any time this testimony is told, written, or shared, that it brings glory to Jesus above all else. We want Him to be glorified and for the all sufficiency of His life, love, and sacrifice to bring salvation, redemption, and eternal hope to humanity to be center stage. Yes! What happened to our daughter really happened, it really changed her, it changed us … but it's because she encountered Him, Jesus is the one who we give all thanks to for the outcome of Abigail's accident! I wanted to ensure that this account would cause people who read it or hear about it to place their hope and trust in a God who sees, hears, knows and is with us, even in the valley of the shadow of death. He is real, He is worthy of our worship and He will walk with you through the victories and the tragedies in every season of your life.

Lastly, I have personally walked through grief and the tragedy of losing someone you love deeply. My prayer, is that as you read this if you have also lost someone, that you would take comfort in the One who dries every tear and exchanges those tears and ashes for beauty. I pray that you would see how well my Abigail was taken care of while she was in Heaven by Jesus and that you would see Jesus as not only a savior but also as a loving, nurturing, protector and friend who cares about the details of our lives right down to Abbey's love for twirling. He is so much better than we could ever imagine and the words in this book will never come close to describing just how incredible He is. To see Him one day will truly be the reward of my life!

Preface

So, please be encouraged as you walk the journey of the following chapters with me, that the very promise of the entirety of God's word still rings true today. God is almighty, He is all knowing, and He is ever-present in every place, His sovereignty and His power are a safe place for all of us who place our trust in His name!

1

Vacation

I f you had the opportunity to meet anyone in the world, who would it be? Your favorite movie star or singer might immediately come to mind when presented with this question. For Abigail, or Abbey as she preferred to be called at the time, a pretty infamous ice princess at the time was the center of her universe and the only person she wanted to meet. After all, what little girl wasn't enamored by the sister princess duo? What better way to fulfill her dream than taking her to the amusement park in southern California which was home to this famous ice princess and letting her meet her in person.

For Abbey's third birthday, in August of 2014, meeting this famous ice princess was at the top of her list! We would watch her and her big sister Faith play for countless hours pretending to be ice princess sisters while they would dress up and run around the house singing famous songs from the movie's soundtrack. Abbey enjoyed being the blonde sister and would often tell me how she also had blonde hair like me. While I knew my child was the complete opposite of me in her skin, hair, and eye coloring (basically she is her daddy's twin). I went along with it, flattered that she wanted to look like me and knowing that every little girl wants to look like their mommy. Needless to say, I was going to do whatever I could as her mom to make this birthday wish happen for my little girl.

As with many American families, we are large and live far away from each other. Most of our vacations as a family, involved visiting family. This particular visit that we were planning was going to be seeing Grandma and Grandpa in Southern California.

I grew up in Southern California and my parents still lived there, so our vacations were like getting a "three for one" special. We get in our "Grandma and Grandpa time," we visit our favorite beach, and then we usually try to go to an amusement park.

Southern California during the month of August is indescribably hot! Actually, when you add in visiting one of the world's most popular theme parks with 50,000+ daily visitors … it can become borderline miserable. It would almost be completely unbearable except for the smiles on the kids' faces and cooling off on the water rides. We decided to go ahead and go (despite the heat) so that we could make Abbey and Faith's dreams come true and celebrate Abbey's birthday while we were there.

We live in Colorado which is either a two hour flight or a seventeen hour drive to get to my parents' house. We usually drive since it's a lot more affordable for our larger family and the bonus was we could bring our small dog with us. After quite a bit of planning and a lot of packing we loaded up our car on a Friday evening and left right as the sun was rising the next day.

Our road trips are typically filled with lots of giggles (a common sound in our home with four girls), road games, many songs sung, and the occasional squabble because someone's leg or elbow is crossing a sibling's invisible boundary. I love our road trips! It allows us time to regroup as a family and talk about anything and everything with seventeen hours to kill. Although the two hour flight is much easier, there is something to be said about the bonding that takes place when you are all squished together in the family minivan for a day and a half!

So many wonderful memories flood my heart and mind when I think of the many road trips we have taken as a family. Yes it could be stressful at times, especially when adding a pup to the mix, but every minute was worth it. Every song we sang, every game we played, every disagreement because someone put their hand or foot on their sister's side of the car or looked at them wrong, every bit of it is ALL worth it.

Jason and I grew up on the opposite sides of the country and in very different geographical settings. I grew up in San Diego California, where going to the beach was more of a sport than a luxury. We monitored the tide and listened to the surf report for the day more than we watched the news. My simple life consisted of going to school, church, the beach, and eating at local SoCal taco shops.

Our summers growing up included about four to five trips to the beach in a week barring we could convince my dad to take us. This usually didn't require much convincing since he was born and raised by the ocean. We hiked a lot in the El Capitan Mountain Range behind our home with our dog Licorice, and we did quite a bit of swimming in our pool for relief from the heat.

When it was off season (water temps were too cold) we fished, caught crabs in the rocks at the bay in San Diego, or I would spend countless hours watching my big brother make skateboard ramps and skate. Being outside and enjoying God's creation was a significant part of my upbringing, especially with the beautiful weather we had year round. I love where I grew up. The people were warm, easy going, and conservative, something that may surprise most people about Southern California. A Lot has changed over the years like, so much of the United States, but when I was growing up it was a good place to raise a family. We aren't all crazy, wild, and rebellious as Hollywood and the movie industry would have most people believe. Community was a big part of the little town I grew up in and everyone helped one another out.

Shoveling snow wasn't a part of my life and snow was only for skiing and enjoying if your family chose to make the trek up into the mountains to a ski resort. It's funny how things change and how God's plans for us sometimes look nothing like what we could have ever thought for ourselves. Who knew many years later I would be raising my children in snowy Colorado.

Jason basically grew up in small town America. If you have ever watched old television programming and remember the quaint little town of Mayberry and all of its charm, that is a pretty close resemblance to the part of Virginia that my husband grew up in. When you step into his town, it's like stepping onto a movie set from yesteryear. It's nestled in the Appalachian Mountains with the cutest downtown I have ever seen. It's a place where my husband can often run into his kindergarten teacher or high school baseball friends at any given time. The same barber that cut his hair at sixteen years old can still be found on Main Street cutting hair and exchanging great conversation with all the local folks. The people that make up this town are intelligent but most choose to live very simply. It's a town where a handshake is good enough and they are known by their character and kindness, not necessarily by their vocation. They are some of the warmest and kindest people I have ever met, and their southern accent is all part of their charm. He grew up playing sports (mainly baseball), playing in the snow, catching fireflies or as he calls them, "lightning bugs," and enjoying his Nanny's home cooked southern meals, going to church, and fishing with his Papaw.

One thing that is the same about our upbringing is the Godly, Christian heritage both Jason and I come from. We both were raised by God fearing parents and Grandparents. We both grew up going to church Sunday, Sunday night, and Wednesday night mid-week service. Church was our community. If we were tired we didn't stay home, mom and dad would just tell us to lay down next to them on the church pew and take a nap. Sports were never scheduled on Sundays and services were as long as they needed to be. Church never felt like a stopwatch was controlling the flow of the service. Somehow we all survived by not eating lunch until one or two pm most Sunday afternoons and we all managed to get up the next day in time for work and school. Those were simpler and better times for sure.

I love that our children get to experience both ways of life.... from coastal living to small town living; both of which shaped and made Jason and I who we are today. In return, this balance of our heritage is now shaping our children.

As we pulled into Grandma and Grandpa's house there was excitement in the air and a few shrills because we had finally arrived. We carried all of our luggage inside, hugged Grandma and Grandpa, and started immediately planning what was first on our itinerary while the girls ran all over their house and backyard exploring every square inch of it.

Each time we came it seemed as if it was all new to them and they acted as though they had never been to my parents' home before. My dad loves to garden and has planted so many different plants and trees and has little walkways that lead to beautiful rose gardens with all kinds of treasures that fill their yard. When visiting Grandma and Grandpa's you never know what you will find...from their golden retriever named Jack to a giant tortoise named Miller.

While the kids played, Grandma made them their favorite French toast breakfast. While we all ate we went over all we had planned for the next several days.

First on everyone's summer wish list was the beach! We woke up the next day and loaded up our van with beach chairs and boogie boards and we were on our way to our favorite beach. We have been taking the girls to this cute little beach in San Diego called Tres Palms since they were newborn babies. Every time we walk out onto the sand all kinds of beautiful memories come to my mind of watching them play in the sand, catch waves, and collect seashells. On this trip, Abbey was learning how to boogie board for the first time with Grandpa and Grandma. She had been looking forward to learning and she was finally able to. Being the youngest of four daughters, she often feels like she is always catching up to all her sisters and she is; she eventually caught a tiny wave with Grandma's help and the smile on her face was priceless. As I stood there and watched her catch a wave over and over again, beaming with happiness, it took me back to when my mom and dad taught me how to boogie board and then surf. Most of my summers were spent right there on the beaches of San Diego, swimming in the water for hours. I remember spending so much time in the ocean catching waves that at night, when I would go to sleep, I could still hear the waves. Those were great memories for sure.

After a long day of being in the California sunshine and a few sunburnt faces, we had the girls pick out a rock, and we loaded up in our car to head back to Grandma and Grandpa's home.

My dad has a tradition that every time he takes a trip to the ocean he picks up a black rock and takes it home as a memory of a good time at the ocean. He says every time he looks and sees all the rocks in his yard he smiles because it reminds him of the fun he had and a wave he caught. I can't help but laugh when thinking about that; to know my dad is to know his love for the ocean. This ritual has now become a loved tradition in our family as well, and the girls have filled our home and yard with black rocks.

Over the next few days, we spent countless hours in the sun swimming, building sand castles, and making lasting memories. Our hearts were full, and our sunburnt faces and salty hair showed proof of the fun we had.

After we rested for a day and allowed our sunburns to heal a little, we packed up for our trip the next day to a local amusement park. That night, I am not sure the girls slept much at all with all the excitement and anticipation they had of meeting their favorite characters and riding their favorite rides.

Five-thirty in the morning came early but with some coffee and Grandma in tow we headed to Anaheim. When we entered the park Abbey and Faith had permanent smiles plastered on their faces while Hannah and Lizzie were skipping ahead with excitement!

As soon as we entered the park and walked down the nostalgic Main Street, Abbey and Faith were beaming with smiles and sweet little giggles as we made our way over to where they could meet the ice princess sisters. We looked at the wait time and gasped! Two hours…WHAT?! A two hour wait just to meet these infamous sisters! The girls' faces instantly dropped in fear they wouldn't get to do it. Jason and I looked at each other and immediately he said, "Well you guys go ride some rides and have fun while I wait in line." He is such a good dad, he would do just about anything for his kids and I love that about him.

So off we went to enjoy some of the rides while our older two girls, Hannah and Lizzie left with Grandma to ride their favorite "big girl" rides. Grandma prefers the kiddie rides but is always a good sport and goes wherever with whoever needs her at the time.

We came back each hour to check on Jason and make sure he was fully stocked with plenty of snacks. Apparently he made friends while he was in line with other dads who were doing the same thing as us. He ended up waiting a total of three hours in line before the girls were able to meet the ice princesses. Three hours in the heat and he did it all for his two little princesses - Abbey and Faith.

As soon as we entered the room where they would meet the princesses, Abbey's face was just priceless. She was smiling from ear to ear as they called her to take her turn. She walked right over to the blonde ice princess, who she adored and then, Abbey just froze! No pun intended. She literally was frozen, or as some call it, she was absolutely star struck. She couldn't say a word and when she opened her mouth nothing came out. Faith spoke up as usual (Faith has never met a stranger) and said, "This is my sister, Abbey, she is shy and I'm Faith, nice to meet you."

We took pictures of Abbey while she stood right next to her favorite princess but she never was able to say a word to her the entire time. We all laughed and explained to the girl playing this princess that she was all Abbey could talk about for the past year but apparently she was star struck.

After we left the meet and greet area, Abbey was upset with herself for not saying more but we assured Abbey that we got some cute pictures with all of them and we were on our way to enjoy the rest of our visit. Later, she went on to meet the sea princess, and there were no problems. In fact we all laughed as Abbey talked her ear off.

The rest of our trip consisted of waiting in long lines, eating churros, enjoying their famous pineapple whips, and watching the parade where we all promise we saw the blonde ice princess wave at Abbey (a birthday wish of hers)!

We ended our time there with a traditional dinner at the chicken restaurant on Main Street. We spent two full days going between the two parks walking many miles and let me tell you, we were worn out. These little girls of ours ran our legs off, and Grandma's too. As always, our time was spent making a lot of great memories with our beautiful daughters, and now we were ready to head back home to my parents' house for the final part of our trip.

The next day, we went over to my childhood friend, Shaunna's house for lunch. We always do whenever we are in town. Shaunna and I grew up together in church and we have been friends since we were about six or seven years old. Our parents were also good friends when we were growing up. Her family is like my family and there aren't too many memories from my childhood that don't include them.

As we watched our kids play and our husbands visit, I remember having a conversation with her about heaven. Out of the blue, she started talking about Heaven and wanted my opinion about some things. She had asked me if I believed families were together in Heaven and had also brought up a recently released movie about heaven. She wanted my opinion and thoughts on the storyline from that movie. I explained how I had only seen the previews but hadn't actually seen the movie or read the book. She didn't doubt the little boy in the least, just wanting my opinion on it.

We continued to talk about Heaven and what we thought it would be like. She and I have had many conversations over our lifetime, but I don't remember us ever talking so intently about this particular topic. Such an interesting and oddly timed conversation for us to have considering in just two short weeks our family would go through something that was exactly what we were talking about.

We spent the next few days exploring San Diego, visiting the lighthouse, searching for sea life in the tide pools of La Jolla, and visiting the smelly (but cute) sea lions. The girls enjoyed long talks with Grandma, singing church songs with Grandpa, and playing fetch with their dog Jack. Jason and I also got our fair share of California sunshine. We drove through the vineyards each morning after getting our coffee at our favorite coffee house and reflected on memories of starting our family there. We would talk about how far God had brought us since we first were married and all that we had gone through and come out of. Jason and I got married and started our family in this town that was lined with beautiful vineyards, championship golf courses, and orange groves. Even though God had moved us, this area will always be so dear to our hearts.

We always tried to reflect on how good God had been to us even through difficult times. He has always been so faithful to our family. These little times of reflection are so important to us and have been an integral part of our family's life. We have taught our girls the importance of praise, even when it seems the storms are rising all around you; praise is our biggest and most unused weapon. These reflections were not just a trip down memory lane but also a chance to praise God for everything, even the hard times He had brought us through.

I know God called us to be pioneers in Colorado, and Colorado has been so good to our family, but anytime we have had to leave family to go back home, it has always stung a bit for us.

Our hearts were full, and our bodies felt rested, but it was time to start our journey back home to Colorado. We woke up early and started our drive back home after Grandma packed snacks for us and Grandpa prayed for safety over us all.

We enjoyed our drive back, but we were all sad that our vacation had come to an end. Our older daughters were dreading going back to school, while our babies (as we still call them to this day because they are the baby girls) were sad to see dad go back to work.

The drive is about seventeen hours with stops but it always seems to be enjoyable with our clan. Faith always sings at the top of her lungs while Hannah makes jokes with her witty sense of humor. Lizzie continuously points out beautiful landscapes we see along the way as our nature lover, while Abbey just takes it all in with a giant smile on her face and the occasional sarcastic and sassy remark to her sisters!

Abbey is our sassy, but at the same time, extremely sensitive child. She is the one who can blurt out something sarcastic to her sisters but as soon as she does she quickly puts her hand over her mouth and says, "I'm so sorry" as her eyes fill up with tears of regret. She can definitely defend herself, and being the youngest of four girls she needs to possess that characteristic as well.

She adores all of her sisters but she especially adores Faith. In Abbey's eyes Faith can do no wrong. To this day Abbey's relationship with her big sister, Faith is one that could stand to be mirrored by many of us with siblings. She clings to her side and defends her fiercely. If Faith is ever unable to complete her homework or do the dishes, Abbey will come to me as her attorney giving me all the reasons why Faith wasn't able to complete the task. The reasons often make me smile because although I don't fall for it for a minute, the loyalty and love she has for Faith makes me thankful.

Faith is equally devoted to Abbey but in a very protective way. She is always making sure Abbey isn't in harm's way and constantly defending her if need be. In a way I think it's why Abbey was so enamored with the ice princesses, because she saw herself and Faith in the story.

2

Home

As we pulled into the driveway of our home in Colorado, we were exhausted from the long drive but excited to finally be home. We unpacked what we could and our heads couldn't hit our pillows fast enough. We were happy to be home and to get settled back into the routine of our everyday lives.

Our lives were busy most days. Jason worked a full time job for a great company while I was a full time mommy. We also both served as youth pastors at a local church.

Being youth pastors was a role we were so very passionate about. We loved ministering to young people. I think no matter what we do for the Lord in our lifetime, outside of raising our children, that our time in youth ministry will always be some of the most cherished memories we have in ministry. These kids made such an impression on our hearts, they changed us. There are no words to possibly express how you feel when you have a young person hand you a razor blade because they have decided they no longer want to harm themselves, or watching them weep at the altar while holding them and praying for them because they were hurting inside as a result of what life had thrown on them. The midnight calls asking us to come to the hospital because one of your youth tried to take their life, those were the hard calls. It wasn't all hard; there were joyous times as well. We enjoyed watching them fall in love with Jesus and see it click that He is so much more than a catch phrase or a Christian shirt they wear. The years of watching them grow spiritually into their identity in Jesus and seeing them mature into their own was worth it all. What we saw in youth ministry was enough to humble and encourage you in the best ways. Young people are amazing and so very underestimated. Youth ministry is not for the faint of heart, it's hard and it requires leaders who are in it for the long haul. I know Jason and I will never be the same again after pastoring such an amazing group of young people. Every single one of them took up a place in our hearts and still does to this day. No matter what roads they took, we love them all the same today as we did back then.

We served with a team of youth leaders that made it possible for us to have four children and a full time job. These youth leaders were also like family to us.

It takes a village to be able to do the Lord's work and also to raise kids. We were thankful for our village and the grace God had given us for this season in our lives.

Even though we were going, at what seemed at the time, a hundred miles an hour I can't ever remember our kids complaining about having to be at the church or having to go to youth events. It simply didn't faze them, it was just their life as ministers' kids.

Our kids have been a part of every ministry we have ever been involved in, which has been our intention from day one. We have always felt, we do it as a family or we don't do it at all. In return, we have watched our girls go out and be little lights and ministers wherever they go. They aren't perfect but they do what we do in the church but in their sphere of influence. My daughter Faith countless times has won someone to the Lord in the dugout at her softball practices. My oldest has been a beacon of light to the hurting at her work, or a voice of truth on controversial topics, which results in peers asking her more about what she believes. Abbey shares her story every chance she gets. She cannot ever back down to unbelief, and Lizzie has been a voice of compassion to the ones overlooked by society. Each one carries their own gifts, but each one has the confidence to be used. They do not need to wait, until they grow up, it's just not how we have raised them.

Life had been busy while we went about with our daily schedules. Days were filled with taking kids back and forth to school, back and forth to the church, and chasing our four little girls around the house. We spent most of our Saturdays hanging out with our girls whether it was a bike ride or going for ice cream. Saturdays were sacred in our home and a day we usually guarded and saved for family time with them.

When we returned home from our California trip, the girls immediately started asking what we were going to do that first Saturday home. Abbey was very much looking forward to graduating from her nursery class on that Sunday and going to preschool class at church, now that she was officially three years old. She had talked about it all summer and was counting down the days. Pastor Debi (our children's pastor) had arranged to bring her and others her age into the 'Little Sparks' class the first Sunday in September.

While we were driving to pick her older sisters up from school, Abbey was talking to me about her Little Sparks class at church that she now would be able to go to. I looked in the rearview mirror at her in her car seat and watched her face light up as she told me all about going into this class. I said to her as we were driving, "Abbey, where does Jesus live?" With her big smile she said, "In my heart, mama." I said, "That's right, Jesus is in your heart." This was a conversation Abbey and I would often have during our drives in the car, and she would always say the same answer with a smile on her face. It was a familiar routine she and I had.

Up until this point in Abbey's life she had heard basic Bible stories, nothing really more than that. She was being raised in a minister's home so her exposure to the things of God and Bible stories was very present, but her understanding was that of someone at her age level. She knew and loved the basics of the Christian faith - Jesus died on the cross and lived in her heart, Jesus was born in a manger to Mary and Joseph in Bethlehem and that is why we celebrate Christmas. Although she loved Jesus, her world was princesses, playing with her baby dolls, and running all over with her sister, Faith. She was very much a typical little girl in every way possible.

We have always raised our children to be children and that included how Jason and I approached teaching them Bible stories. We never pushed deep things on them when they weren't ready for it. We wanted them to enjoy the stories of Noah's ark and Adam and Eve and all the coloring pages, vacation Bible school songs, and Sunday school puppet shows that went with those stories. Children these days are growing up way too fast and we want ours to enjoy every stage of childhood without the pressure to grow too quickly.

The week had come to an end and we were getting ready to settle into the weekend and enjoy time off together as a family. Abbey was jumping up and down saying, "Two more days and I get to go to pweeschool at church!" Abbey's vocabulary and understanding was well advanced for her age, she had the cutest way of pronouncing the letters "L" and "R" as "W's" and we loved it.

Her advanced understanding and vocabulary may have been because she had three older sisters and she learned from them in order to keep up with them. It also could have been from the need to make her voice known in a house with three older sisters who were always talking. Whatever the reason, people often commented on how well she spoke and how much she understood and comprehended at her age.

Everyone in our home settled into bed and Abbey wanted to sleep with us that night so we let her. She brought me her favorite book that I would always read to her entitled, "Are You My Mother?" Abbey and I have a joke between us about her looking nothing like me but being just like me at the same time. While I love all my daughters equally, Abbey is my mini-me in every way imaginable, except in the way she looks.

Like I mentioned earlier she is her daddy's twin through and through. At this age she wanted to look like me so she would often say, "Mama I have bwonde hair just like you." It is probably why she was so obsessed with the blonde ice princess. Abbey has dark brown hair and the prettiest green eyes with a beautiful dark olive complexion. I have blonde hair, blue eyes and fair skin. We couldn't be more opposite. We would joke back and forth while reading this book and she would always laugh these huge belly laughs as we flipped through the pages. I would say to her, "Is the mama bird your mama?" She would just laugh and laugh. I would always end the book with, "Abbey, who's your mother?" She would then answer, "You are mama." She would wrap her sweet little arms around my neck and give me a kiss goodnight and then settle into bed. It was something she and I did and it was something I treasured.

Daddy prayed for all of us and we all headed to bed. Little did we know what tomorrow would bring for our family. The following day would challenge us, stretch our faith, test the depths of our beliefs in Jesus, heaven, angels, and eternity. Everything was about to change in the best and worst kind of ways.

3

The Accident

Saturday, September 06, 2014, started out just like any other day. We can all remember exactly what we were doing that day because it turned out to be anything but ordinary. I was running on the treadmill in our bedroom upstairs; Hannah, our oldest, was cleaning her clarinet; Lizzie, Faith and Abbey were all watching cartoons in our living room while eating cereal, and Jason was getting ready to go for a run in our neighborhood.

This Saturday was a turning point for our family. It was a day where we would never be the same again. That may sound dramatic, but Abbey's accident really did impact us that drastically. Our understanding of God the Father was about to be radically changed. Our understanding of Heaven was about to become so much more than what we had learned up to this point in our lives. This was a day where the faith we loved, lived, and preached was about to be tested.

It is one thing to trust God for daily provision, but quite another thing to trust God to raise your child from the dead and heal her. It is in those moments, the moments that test everything you know and believe, where you grow closer to Him, no matter the outcome. The Bible says that it is in our moments of weakness that Jesus' power is made perfect (2 Corinthians 12:9). A statement we can readily acknowledge after the fact, but would have been difficult to fully understand in the moment we were about to walk through.

Jason had decided to go for a run outside while I was running on the treadmill upstairs. Whenever Jason leaves to go anywhere the girls run after him to say goodbye or to beg him to let them go with him. It had become a small and sweet habit of theirs. They love their daddy, there is no mistaking that.

This day was no exception, and as soon as they heard the garage door open Lizzie and Abbey were up on their feet and running fast after him.

Lizzie ran down the hallway with Abbey following right behind her. Lizzie swung the door leading to the garage open and ran down the three steps that led to the concrete garage floor. This was no ordinary door. In Colorado, unlike many states, the door that leads from the garage to the home has to be self-closing and have some fire resistance. It was very heavy. As Lizzie ran after her daddy, she assumed Abbey made it out to the garage with her before the door slammed shut. Abbey hadn't. It's important to note Lizzie was only eight years old, and remembering to make sure the door didn't shut on Abbey wasn't in the forefront of her mind. This was something she beat herself up for later even though we told her she did nothing wrong. Abbey attempted to head down the stairs right behind Lizzie when that heavy fire proof, extra-weighted garage door slammed shut on her wrist!

Abbey had a medical condition that first presented itself in her when she was six months old. This condition is called, *"Cyanotic-breath holding spell."* At six months old, she was swinging in her baby swing when her sister Faith had tried to pick her up out of the swing to hold her, and she dropped her just about eight inches off the ground onto the carpet. She wasn't hurt in any way but it made Abbey so upset at six months old that she held her breath and then passed out. I found out later when I took her to our local Children's Hospital Urgent Care that she had this breath-holding condition. The pediatrician explained it as basically a bad temper. She said what happens when they get so upset or they get hurt, they hold their breath and pass out. It wasn't life threatening, and I shouldn't worry about it, but expect it to happen many more times before she would grow out of it. The doctor had said to expect her to grow out of it by seven or eight years old.

Abbey held true to the pediatrician's comments and had many more of those incidents as she grew older and all were when she was upset or hurt. It became a condition we all were very familiar with, and would try to look out for in Abbey. Every time this happened, we would blow gently in her face or pinch her little heel lightly and she would wake up almost immediately.

Lizzie looked back and saw Abbey at the top of the stairs holding her little wrist. She was holding her breath about to scream as she had done so many times in the past. Knowing Abbey usually passed out when she got hurt, Lizzie screamed out to Jason, "Daddy, it's Abbey, she is hurt!" Lizzie ran over to Abbey as quickly as she could but it was too late. Abbey had held her breath, passed out and fell down the three stairs onto the concrete floor. She was unconscious so she had nothing to break her fall. Jason turned around where he had been tying his running shoes on the driveway, and headed toward her. As with most accidents this all happened in seconds not minutes, so he was unable to get to her in time. Her head hit the concrete floor with a loud crack.

Abbey's body slid, landing under the front bumper of our minivan with her head facing up. Her delicate head bounced up and down, hitting the underside of the front bumper. Her little body began to have a seizure because of her head smacking the garage floor with such great force. We were told later by the doctors that often with head injuries, a seizure or even a stroke can happen because of the sudden impact and subsequent trauma caused to the brain.

Watching his baby girl's head bounce up and down, hitting

The Accident

the bumper, and knowing he couldn't do anything was his worst nightmare, both as a protector and as a father. It was a moment in time where he literally had to put every bit of his trust in the One who gave us Abbey and just hold onto that hope. Jason explained to me that he felt like throwing up as he watched our little girl going through this. He said it felt like eternity trying to get to her while she was having a seizure.

He ran to pick her up, remembering to be extremely careful with her neck. He scooped her up and held her close to him as he ran into the house. After he picked her up, he felt Abbey's body go from slightly tense to completely limp. When Jason felt her little body go limp, he carefully leaned her face back away from laying on his shoulder, and he saw her lips begin to turn blue and then the blue began to spread all around her mouth. He had his finger on her very faint pulse until it was no more.

He headed in the house and up the stairs to our room, where I was running on the treadmill. As he ran up the stairs, he screamed my name over and over again, "SARAH! SARAH! SARAH!" He continued to hold his fingers on her neck, checking for her pulse and he noticed now that all of her breathing movements in her chest had also stopped. Her pulse was gone, her breathing was stopped, and that is when he entered our room and laid her out on our bed. I jumped off the treadmill quickly and Jason, with extreme panic in his shaky voice, screamed, "Abbey fell…she hit her head…and she is…I think she is dead!"

How do I even come close to explaining what my heart felt in that moment as I heard those words come from my husband's mouth while staring at my littles girl's lifeless body sprawled out on our bed? I can't. If you are a parent who has gone through trauma with your child you understand there are no words - just emotions, tears, heartache, and fear. Yes, I said fear. As a believer in Jesus, fear can be a bad word, but if I am being real and raw, fear is what entered into my heart immediately. Fear is a human emotion that is very real and to pretend that it's not is ignorance.

Almost as fast as fear entered into my heart, faith flooded it even more. I don't want to give the impression that we are these amazing faith-filled individuals because we aren't. We are just ordinary people who love Jesus, and believe He is good no matter the outcome. We do struggle at times with our human emotions. When fear tried to overtake me, I prayed and asked God to help me. Nothing fancy and elaborate, just simply, "God help us, please!"

I can't explain what happened, but it's like the Lord just blanketed me with His peace and anointed me with His direction. I instantly had a calmness and clarity of mind when I should have been in a state of hysteria. I was upset and worried, but I knew what to do at that moment, and I didn't fall apart. I told my girls who were screaming and crying to stop panicking and to start praying.

Jason looked at me in a state of shock and said, "What do I do?" Before I could even think about what I was saying I shouted, "Do CPR on her!" Jason immediately started praying and asking God to guide him. He said what happened next was nothing short of humbling and a miracle all wrapped up in one. He said he instantly saw a vision of himself performing CP on Abigail and so he followed the images he was seeing played out before his eyes.

I have to say as an onlooker, he had an incredible calmness yet urgency about him. While he was performing CPR on her I was trying my best to speak with the 911 dispatch operator.

When the 911 operator answered my call, she asked me how long Abbey had been without a pulse and I answered her, "I am not sure, maybe 3-4 minutes but I don't know."

When the operator on the phone asked me for my address I didn't know it, this is how much shock I was in. She said, "Ma'am, I cannot track you from your cell phone. Is there a landline you can use?" I quickly answered that we didn't have a landline, and I screamed for my ten year old daughter, Hannah to come and help me. She came into the room, and she quickly told me our address and I gave it to the operator. I felt very strongly that I was not to not wait for the ambulance to come to our home but to take Abbey ourselves to the emergency room. I told the operator that the closest emergency room was 15 minutes away and I just didn't want to wait for the ambulance to arrive. She agreed with me on this course of action and even said she would let the ambulance know when we were on our way so they could meet us on the road.

The operator stayed on the phone with Hannah while I was trying my best to count how long Abbey was without a heartbeat. Jason continued to perform CPR on Abbey while we all just waited, watched, and prayed. I wish I could say I fought this hard battle by praying and contending, but there wasn't time for that. I just said, "I trust you, God. You do what only You can do." It was a quick and simple prayer but from a deep place of desperation. After several attempts, I saw her little chest breathe a breath, and we instantly felt a little bit of relief and hope. Jason screamed with tears, "I have a heartbeat, I have a heartbeat!" Right then I thought to myself, God Himself breathed His breath of life into my little girl's lungs. I was reminded while writing this of how it must have looked on that day God first created man. He literally breathed into His nostrils the breath of life and man became a living soul (Genesis 2:7). Here we were, needing Him to do the same thing to Abbey as He did when He created man and He did! I quickly told the 911 operator she was now breathing and she said to me, "Good now head to the emergency room and I will call the ambulance and let them know to meet you on the road."

She instructed me (I was going to be driving) to drive as fast as I could safely drive and to honk my horn to get people to move out of the way. She emphasized to me that seconds matter and that she needs oxygen as soon as possible because her brain was without it for a good amount of time.

4

She Speaks

Once Jason was able to get a steady pulse he scooped her up in his arms and we jumped into the car to head to the hospital. Even though Abbey's heart was beating, her breaths were very shallow and her body was trying to shut down again. Her eyes were faintly open and dilated, and her heart was beating but she wasn't there. She would stare out into space and she would stare right through us. The best way to describe her state of being at this point was that she had a heartbeat but there was no "life" in her. Her sweet little smiling self just wasn't there. She wasn't speaking and she didn't appear conscious even though her eyes were open for brief, little moments. We both have our "guesses" as to how long Abbey was gone without a heartbeat but we don't know for sure. We weren't looking at a watch, we were just trying to get her heart to beat! I had counted around four minutes when Jason started CPR but there were a few minutes before that where she was gone. If we had to estimate it was possibly around seven to eight minutes total.

We were on our way to the hospital with our girls and Jason was in the front seat holding onto Abbey. He said to me that we needed to get there as soon as possible because her pulse was faint and she was struggling to breathe consistently.

I drove as fast as I could do so safely. I would honk and wave my arms out the window screaming, "Move please emergency!" While we were driving I will never forget the sound of my little girls in the back seat praying and crying their little eyes out for their little sister. It was a sweet moment in the middle of a storm for our family.

As I drove, Jason would pinch her heel and blow in her face to get her to breathe whenever she would stop. I remember him very loudly saying over and over again, "Abbey, Abbey wake up!" Then he would just pray over her lifeless body and say, "Oh God help us, we need a miracle." She continued to stare lifelessly into nowhere. The thoughts that raced through both of our minds were that she is alive (barely) but she is brain dead. I remember thinking about how different our life would be from this point on and almost immediately I would say to myself, "NO, NO! That's not going to happen!" I would literally take those thoughts captive and throw them out of my mind. I was praying, my girls were praying and tears were streaming down our faces. We didn't know why this was happening but all we could do was trust in the One who gave us Abbey to begin with.

About halfway to the emergency room everything changed regarding Abbey. I would call this miracle number two in her story although looking back there were many little miracles that happened throughout that day. Jason continually tried to get her to breathe steadily by talking to her and blowing in her face. He was so desperate, as we all were, to see the little life he had once known, protected, and loved, come back to us.

Then suddenly Abbey spoke! While Jason was saying her name over and over again she suddenly looked at him with her beautiful, sparkly green eyes and said very faintly, "Daddy?" With tears of joy he answered, "Yes honey, I'm here." She said to him, "Where is mommy?" We all started to cry tears of unimaginable joy! I said, "I am right here baby." Jason explained to her that I was driving and that she had had an accident. He told her we were on our way to the hospital to get her all taken care of. He assured her he had her and she didn't need to be afraid.

We have marked in our hearts that it was here, halfway to the emergency room where God sent our Abigail Joy back to us. Yes it was on our bed where her heart began to beat again but it was in the front seat of our car that her spirit, her life was returned to us. I can't theologically explain it; it's just what we experienced. Our Abbey spoke, she saw us and recognized us and we just knew everything else we would face God would see us through just as He had up until this point.

As we were approaching the emergency room I dropped Jason and Abbey off at the front entrance while I went to park. I called my sister, who lived close by and asked her to meet us at the emergency room so she could pick up our girls. I also asked her to pray. I had already called my parents and quickly told them Abbey had an accident and they needed to pray. I jumped off the phone and ran inside to meet Jason and Abbey with our girls in tow.

Later my dad shared with me that when he and my mom hung up with me on the phone they immediately had a prayer meeting for Abbey. My uncle happened to be visiting my parents at the time and he was away from the Lord. My dad said he felt a tremendous travail come over him and my mom and they just fell to their knees with my uncle joining them crying out to God for Abbey's healing. Later when my uncle heard Abbey's story he went on to re-dedicate his life to the Lord and ended up sharing Abbey's story with many others. It touched him in a way that caused him to turn back to the Lord.

When I walked into the emergency room I saw Jason holding Abbey and what appeared to be him arguing with the lady at the front desk. She had wanted Jason to fill out quite a bit of paperwork before they would see Abbey. Jason was explaining to her that Abbey had died and we resuscitated her and that Abbey needed oxygen as soon as possible and that the 911 operator was supposed to have called ahead to let them know we would be arriving. The lady working at the front desk said no one called and she needed him to sit down and fill out the paperwork. A sweet lady standing in line behind Jason and Abbey said, "Let them go back! We all can wait, you heard him… she needs oxygen!" The lady at the front desk still would not budge and even went as far as to say that Abbey looked fine to her. Right then a dear friend of ours named Chris, who worked there in the emergency room as a nurse, walked by with his lunch in his hands. Chris went to church with us and was also one of our youth leaders. I was entering the ER when Chris was walking by and he said to me, "Sarah, what's wrong?" With a quivering voice I said, "It's Abbey she had an accident and she died and she….she… needs oxygen." He immediately put his lunch down and quickly intervened letting the lady at the front desk know he had it taken care of from then on. He took us and Abbey back immediately to get her on oxygen.

My sister arrived and she hugged our necks, kissed Abbey on the forehead and took our other daughters back home with her. She said with tears as she left with the girls, "I'm praying."

While Abbey was receiving oxygen and we were waiting on the results of the tests and scans she vomited a few times. They said that was normal for people with brain injuries and concussions. The doctor was hesitant to say what was going on until he ran more tests on her but he said she probably suffered one of those. While she was sitting there in her bed she didn't look good at all. She was awake and she knew who we all were but she just wasn't well. She looked sick and overall she looked like she was hurting.

While she lay there in the hospital bed I held her hand with tears streaming down my face. Just like so many times before when I would read to her our favorite story, I whispered in her ear, "Abbey, who's your mother?" She looked up at me with these sad eyes and faintly answered, "You are mama." I was never so happy to hear her say that to me as I was right in that moment. That was all I needed. To know my baby girl remembered. It gave me such a hope that we would get through this.

The doctor came into the room where we were waiting eagerly. They had received back some of the results of her tests and scans. I'll never forget the way the doctor looked when he entered our room. He looked like what he had to say was going to be hard to say and difficult for us to hear. I could tell it wasn't good news by his countenance and body language. Some would say this is false because doctors are used to sharing bad news but if a doctor ever comes to the place where he is emotionless when delivering bad news then he has lost the reason for becoming a doctor. This was not the case with this doctor. He was kind and he obviously cared.

The doctor explained that he had called a critical care ambulance to take her immediately to Children's Hospital in Aurora. At first I didn't understand him when he said an ambulance would take her so I asked him if we could take her ourselves. He responded with, "No she needs to be monitored and she needs to get there quickly." I could tell he was hesitant to say much. He was holding back and I could feel it. Both Jason and I were at a loss for words. I asked a million questions but he did not want to answer any of them. He said he would feel more comfortable having the pediatric neurological team at Children's answer our questions and explain to us what was going on with Abbey. He also explained he had already sent over her scans to them and had spoken with the head of the neuro team that was on call that day. I asked him to tell me if this was a concussion and he said no it's more serious than that.

At that moment fear came over me like a flood again. A neuro team? I thought to myself "No, we just got her back!" It seemed that for every step forward we would take ten steps backward. Among the many questions we asked while waiting for the ambulance to arrive, one of the questions that Jason asked the doctor was if what we experienced with Abbey was indeed that she actually died. He answered yes and said it was very smart that he performed CPR on Abbey because it's what saved her life. He explained that sadly so many don't know how to do that and many lives could be saved if people just performed CPR when a head injury occurs.

The ambulance arrived and ironically they made a comment

while loading Abbey onto their stretcher. They said to us, "We got this call to meet you all on the road but we didn't end up coming because we were tied up." I was upset at first but then I realized it confirmed why I felt the Holy Spirit lead me to take her to the emergency room myself and to not wait for an ambulance.

I kissed Abbey goodbye before they loaded her into the ambulance and told her daddy would be right there by her side and she had nothing to fear. To be honest Abbey looked like she was in pain and she just didn't really care what was going on around her. This made me all the more nervous. Jason and I agreed to have him go with her in the ambulance while I went home to grab some clothes and then I would meet them at Children's Hospital. The doctor encouraged me to pack for a week at least. That comment also didn't help my fears.

5

Ezekiel 16:6

Jason and Abbey arrived at the hospital and a team of pediatric doctors and nurses from the neuro care team met them and immediately assessed her. The head neurosurgeon that was on call came into Abbey's room and spoke to Jason. He explained that the overall situation with Abbey wasn't looking good and that her scans showed significant bleeding on her brain. He explained how they would most likely need to operate to relieve the pressure on her brain but before they would do that they would observe and assess her for a period of time and if she didn't pass certain cognitive tests they would then proceed to operate. The surgeon introduced Jason and Abbey to his team who would be evaluating her and then he left. Jason said the neurosurgeon was extremely informative and compassionate and he was thankful that he and his team to be working with Abbey.

Over the next hour the team proceeded to do a series of cognitive tests on Abbey and she was not passing them. She refused popsicles, movies, and failed every single cognitive test they did with her.

She just wanted to sleep and not be bothered. While her daddy sat there with her he told me that even though she was conscious she just looked so sick, which really concerned him.. He began to worry as he watched the team come in and perform tests, trying to get her to engage in conversation, or to point to items they would hold up. She failed all of the tests. They then would walk out of the room with a look of deep concern on their faces. He knew what that meant. He knew she was dangerously close to having to have a major surgery done that may or may not be successful, and may or may not have lifelong side effects.

On my way to the hospital, I received a phone call from Jason. When I answered he said to me, "Sarah" and then there was just silence on the other end of the phone. At first I thought the service was bad, but it wasn't. He was struggling to tell me what was going on with Abbey. I frantically said "Jason what's wrong?" He paused and I could tell he was fighting tears when he said to me, "It's not good." I asked him what was going on and he encouraged me just to get there as soon as I could. With a very panicked voice I said, "Please tell me now what's wrong, I don't want to wait…..tell me now please!" He said, "It's her brain, she has a significant bleed on it and they are most likely going to operate on her. She isn't responding to them very well. She is just lying in the bed, she has taken a turn for the worse, just get down here!" I begged him to please have them wait until I got there if they could, but if not, I understood and I would be there as soon as I could.

When I got off the phone I felt this lump in my throat and sickness enter my stomach. It was all I could do to not pass out. I cried many tears on that long car ride to the hospital. I felt this fight rise up within me, it wasn't much of a fight but with whatever faith I had left in me I prayed, and I prayed from the deepest parts of me. As I drove I prayed, "PLEASE don't take her again PLEASE!!! You gave her back to us, please let us keep her!"

While Jason was there in the room with Abbey waiting he had posted a request to social media asking people to pray for her. A few minutes after posting that he received a text message from a family friend saying she was praying and she felt led to share this scripture with him in Ezekial 16:6 "And when I passed by you and saw you struggling in your own blood, I said to you in your blood, 'Live!" Yes, I said to you in your blood, 'Live!"

Jason read the scripture on his phone to himself and he said he heard the Lord say to him, "Pray that scripture out loud over your daughter." He then began to pray Ezekiel 16:6 over Abbey. As soon as he finished praying he said that's when he witnessed yet another miracle in our precious little girl. This was our third and final miracle. Abbey sat up in her hospital bed and turned to Jason and said, "Daddy, can I have a popsicle?" He looked at her in amazement and knew that his vibrant little girl with sparkly green eyes had come back....FULLY. He hugged her and said, "Of course you can baby!" Jason called the nurse back in and asked if she would get Abbey a popsicle. When the nurse came in, Abbey asked her if she could also watch a movie. The nurse was surprised; she also was witnessing the complete turnaround in Abbey. The nurse let Jason know this was a very good sign and that she would go get the neuro surgeon so he could evaluate her again.

While they waited for the doctor to come back Jason and Abbey were watching a movie and in typical Jason fashion he wanted to ask her a bunch of questions to evaluate her for himself. Jason is our protector in every way, he always has been the one who takes care of us all when we are sick, tending to our every need whether it's praying for us, taking our temperature, giving us medicine or just comforting us. We have joked in our family that he missed his calling in life and that he should have been a doctor because of his love for anything that is medically related. He researches medical topics for fun and thinks of things we don't regarding symptoms. Overall he just seems to understand the human body and all of its many functions in a way the average person does not. He does not ever claim to be a doctor and when he is put in front of one he asks them more questions than they probably want. I don't think I have ever met someone who hates sickness as much as he does. He will often say "Jesus hated sickness and destroyed it, so we should hate sickness and ask Him to destroy it every chance we get!" If you know Jason well you know his hate for sickness runs deep! Hand sanitizers are in every car and personal hygiene and an overall carefulness have always been top on his list. Me, I am more of a "germs are good for you and it's ok to run around barefoot" person. We balance each other out.

Jason turned to Abbey and asked her this simple question that would in many ways change our lives forever. He looked at her wanting to know if she had any degree of amnesia and asked, "Abbey, do you remember what happened to you? Do you know why we are here in the hospital?" Abbey stopped watching the movie and looked at him and said, "Yes I do, Faith slammed my wrist in the door (Faith actually didn't do this but we thought it was a typical little sister thing to blame it on her big sister) and I was on the ground under mommy's van. Two really big men (she used her hands to attempt to show how tall they were) bigger than Papa (Jason's dad is a tall man) came and they took me to heaven." She then looked at Jason and with great excitement said, "Daddy! Did you know Jesus is God?" Jason perked up as Abbey continued to explain, "When I went to Heaven I met Jesus and He told me He was God and that I was going to be ok. He is so nice, daddy."

Jason sat there in disbelief as he listened to her tell the account of what she remembered. Abbey told him how she saw someone we used to go to church with who had recently passed away a few months prior to this. She explained how she wore a beautiful necklace around her neck. We spoke to the family of the girl who Abbey saw, her mom told me her daughter loved necklaces and asked for one the last birthday she had with them. We were not close to the family or the girl who had passed. We knew her from our interactions at church and prayed for her healing of cystic fibrosis and we were there at the hospital trying to comfort her and her family as she passed but we weren't super close to her, unfortunately. To Jason it was odd that Abbey saw her since this young lady wasn't someone who Abbey was close to. Abbey only said a few short sentences about her trip to Heaven and then she was done talking about it and back to watching her movie.

Jason sat there in disbelief of what she had just shared with him. Not disbelief of her story but just complete and total disbelief of the moment itself.

I quickly jumped out of my car and ran up to the hospital room where Abbey and Jason were. They were in a special area of the hospital and in a private room that was for neuro patients who were being observed and undergoing tests.

When I got there, Abbey was up and watching a movie. She said to me with so much excitement, "Hi mama!" I felt so confused but extremely hopeful all at the same time. What Jason shared with me on the phone to what I was seeing with my own eyes was dramatically different. Jason looked at me and explained how he had prayed that scripture over her and almost immediately after praying for her that she was herself again. He explained that they were waiting for her neuro team to come in and evaluate her again.

I had instant tears of joy! I was so thankful and hopeful. I sat down in the room and felt for the first time over the last twelve hours that I could actually exhale. I thought to myself what a whirlwind of emotions we just went through and things were looking very hopeful!

While we were waiting Jason looked at me and said, "Sarah, Abbey said something to me about what happened to her when she….when she…when she had her accident." I could tell neither of us wanted to say the words of what actually happened out loud. He had asked and confirmed with the doctor in the emergency room at the hospital she was transported from and that was hard enough.

He began to tell me everything she had told him about going to Heaven and meeting Jesus. I sat there in disbelief with tears streaming down my face. The emotions were real and very different than what one would think they should be.

I wasn't excited about what she had said and getting my pen out to write down what she had described wasn't what came to my mind. You may be reading this and thinking what is wrong with her? Why on earth would you not be excited about your daughter talking about her going to heaven? The best way I can answer that would be that I am a human with real human emotions. Not everyone is the same and not everyone processes things like this in the same way.

She died and came back. Those are the feelings and emotions we were processing through. Going to Heaven was wonderful to hear but my heart was just trying to get through the fact that she was going to be ok. Until you go through it it's hard to understand what a parent could be feeling in that moment. We sat there feeling as though we had just gone through a washing machine of emotions. Nothing prepared us to hear what she was sharing.

One thing about Jason and I is that we are as real as real gets. Sometimes we make people uncomfortable with how real we are and that's ok. So our account of this isn't made up or exaggerated; it's what we walked through as a family, the good, the bad and the not so pretty versions of ourselves. We understand there will be some who don't believe and that's perfectly fine. What we do hope to accomplish with sharing this testimony of Abbey's encounter with Jesus is to provide hope and comfort because that's what it did for us, it gave us hope and comfort when we didn't even realize we needed it.

As Jason continued to share with me what Abbey had shared with him I remained quiet. I sat there with all of these emotions going through my heart and mind. I looked at him and said, "Wow, that's a lot to take in, I don't even know what to say." I looked at Abbey and asked her to tell me for herself what happened to her. She wouldn't, all she said to me was, "Daddy told you."

I wasn't disappointed because my mind just didn't have the space to even process that right then so instead I said to her, "Well then let's just focus on you getting better so we can go home." She smiled and just returned to watching her movie.

6

Discharged

Over the next few hours the neurosurgeon and his team came around and evaluated Abigail. The Doctor looked at us and said, "Well she is eating, that is a great sign and a huge step forward." He explained how he wasn't ready to say she is out of the woods just yet without doing some more tests but he was very pleased with her sudden improvement. Over the next twenty-four hours we had a team of doctors come in and out of our room to do many tests on Abbey.

Jason and I were able to stay in a room with her where there were two beds. I was thankful for that because there was no way I was leaving her side. I had my baby back and I would sleep on the cold, hard hospital floor if it meant being right by her side. I had Abbey sleep in one of the beds with me while I held her so close to me (probably a little too tight).

We didn't get much sleep because they came in so often to do tests but I remember it was one of the best nights of my life. I had an overwhelming peace in my heart and the presence of the Holy Spirit filled our little hospital room.

Sunday morning came and Abbey was up bright and early and smiling from ear to ear. The doctors had asked her to color some pictures for them and she did perfectly.

Sunday afternoon around four or five o'clock the neurosurgeon came in with his team and a big smile on his face. He said they were discharging her and letting her go home. He told us how very lucky we were. He explained that Abbey had suffered a brain injury but that she had recovered remarkably with no need for surgery. He told us she was a walking miracle and we had a lot to be thankful for. We knew that but we also knew why. Jesus had completely healed our baby girl and we were thankful and humbled by the goodness of God.

When Abbey came into this hospital by ambulance she had bleeding on her brain and she was failing every single test they gave her; then after her dad prayed for her, she was passing every single test with flying colors. God answered us in our time of need and we were so grateful. This is not something that is unique and only available to Jason and I, the anointing and presence of the Holy Spirit is available to people all around the world and when they pray with faith in the name of Jesus and under the authority of Jesus, miracles can happen to the glory of His mighty name!

Even though the doctor was releasing her he was doing so reluctantly because of how soon it was after her accident. He was willing to allow her to go home with us as long as we followed his instructions. He instructed us that if she had any signs of what he listed out on the discharge papers to call and immediately come back in. We were so excited, so relieved and so exhausted but we were ready to go home and be reunited with the rest of our girls.

I can't explain why or how God did it, except to say that He tells us in His Word through the Prophet Isaiah that He bore stripes on and in His body for our healing and that is just what He did for Abbey. He healed her completely. There is no other explanation for what happened to Abigail other than God stepped into the situation and He healed her. The power of His Spirit raised our baby up to restore her to our family and to bring glory to Jesus Christ.

I have tasted grief before so I am aware that some parents do not get the same outcome as we did. I think the hardest part of sharing Abbey's story and writing this book is knowing that there will be those who read this book who did not get the same ending we did and that grieves me..

When I was a young teenage girl I lost my older brother who I was very close to. My family and I walked through a very hard season filled with grief and heartache. It took my family many years to heal from his death and even now there isn't a time when I think about him where I don't start to tear up. Death is hard and I don't think we ever fully lose the ache that death leaves behind, we just learn how to live with it by leaning into the strength of the Lord. We learn that this world is just a brief moment in comparison to eternity.

What my family had to walk through was hard and left us with what seemed to be shattered hearts. I honestly didn't think we would recover from his death, then Jesus came in and healed our brokenness. He literally picked us up out of our pit called grief and He set us on a new foundation that wasn't broken. He poured His oil over us for our mourning and He made us smile again. Only He could have done this. Because He conquered death and because He holds those keys there is healing for the loss of a loved one and there is full restoration. I know because my family is proof, it seemed impossible to ever be normal again or recover from what we walked through but we did.

The thought of someone reading this and thinking God must love us more because He gave us our Abbey back hurts me to the core. The Bible assures us that God is not a respecter of persons and His ways and thoughts are higher than ours. I did not understand why we lost my brother when we did and I asked God a million times why he wasn't healed. I do not know the answers to those questions but I do know that God was faithful to heal, restore and renew our family when no other person could. He put us back together again. He took our ashes that death left us with and exchanged them for beauty just as Isaiah chapter 61 promises.

Without God's amazing grace and restoration my family and I would still be broken in a million pieces, so I do understand the pain and the void that death leaves behind.

As I get into the part of this story where Abbey describes Jesus and Heaven I pray that as you read this you will feel the presence of God and that you have a greater understanding of His heart and love for you. He is an infinitely good Father. He is our friend. He is our comforter and He is an ever present help in a time of need. If you give Him your brokenness He will restore you.

As we arrived back home, my sister was there with my other girls waiting with a giant princess balloon and a matching ice princess doll. If you know my sister you know she is their favorite aunt among many great aunts, but she is the one who loves and spoils them to no end. She is always there for them and she is one of their biggest cheerleaders in life. They are blessed to have her and so am I.

Abbey was so excited to see her sisters and the feeling was mutual. They all ran and attacked her as we walked in the door. Many tears of joy flowed down all of our faces that evening. We ate dinner while we all sat around enjoying our Abbey and not taking another second for granted. Still to this day I look at Abbey and all of my children and thank God for His mercy. I never want to take anything He has done for us for granted.

The next morning Abbey was getting dressed and she began to throw up, so I quickly called her doctor. After many questions he came to the conclusion that she didn't need to come back in unless she threw up more than three times in 24 hours. As the day went on she threw up one other time and that was it. Other than that she was fine with no other side effects. In fact to this day Abbey has had no other breath holding incidents, the one she had with her accident was the last one she had again.

Jason and I felt very confident with a few days behind us after her accident that she was going to be just fine. I also had her story of going to Heaven looming in the back of my mind. Did this really happen? The Bible does say, "To be absent from the body is to be present with the Lord Jesus." These were all thoughts that flooded my mind.

Jason had very different thoughts and emotions towards it all. He avoided hearing Abbey's story if he could without her knowing it. He was so angry at what had happened that he had a hard time admitting that she actually died. There was a very real struggle at work with post traumatic stress syndrome in Jason which was understandable. He only wanted to focus on the fact that she was here with us and safe in our home.

That Sunday evening shortly after we had gotten home when we were getting ready to go to sleep, I asked him if we should ask her again to tell us what happened. His response was immediately, no. I asked him why we shouldn't and he just said when she was ready she would tell us more. I left it with that and agreed to let it go for now.

We settled into bed with Abbey in our bed and in my arms. I wasn't ready to let her go from my grasp. I needed to feel her next to me and I needed to rest my hand on her back and feel her breathing. Faith also joined us because she needed to sleep next to her sissy. Faith was so shaken up about everything that had happened and if being crowded in our bed meant her heart felt settled then that was fine with us.

7

All Better Boo Boos

Monday morning came and we were back into the swing of things. I dropped the older two girls off at school and Jason went to work. That afternoon Faith and Abbey were playing when I called them to the table to eat their lunch. We prayed over our meal and after we were done praying Abbey said, ``Mama did you know Jesus has all better boo boos?" I replied with, "Really? What do you mean by that?" She said, "You know how we call our boo boos that are healed all better boo boos?" She pointed to a scar on my arm I had at the time from burning myself with a curling iron and she said, "Like your all better boo boo mama."

    I looked intently at the scar on my arm and thought about what she was saying for a moment. I looked across the table at her and said to her, "Tell me about all better boo boos that Jesus has." Abbey began to tell me about how Jesus showed her his scars on his hands and feet. She stopped for a second, looked down as if she was collecting her thoughts and said He has them all over His face and she made a circular motion with her little hand across her face.

I immediately thought about the scripture in Isaiah 52:14 that says, *"Just as there were many who were appalled at him his appearance was so disfigured beyond that of any human being and his form marred beyond human likeness."* Jesus was unrecognizable but how did Abbey know that? We had never talked about Jesus having scars on His face and I knew we hadn't gone into detail about His crucifixion because she was so young. I didn't even allow my children to see the movie "The Passion of the Christ" until they were much older because I didn't want to upset their little hearts.

What Abbey had just shared with me had caused me to think about how we grow up with this Sunday school picture of Jesus in our mind. He is the long hair, bearded, Jewish man with these scars in his hands and feet and that's the image we carry around in our mind. This Jesus my daughter was describing was so much more than that. Even the way she described why Jesus showed her His scars moved me to tears. What He did for us was anything but pretty and nothing about Him was basic including His death.

I'll never forget the way she told me what she said next and her concerned sweet voice she said it in. She said, "Mama, Did you know Jesus got those boo boos for our sins? He died on the cross for our sins; He did all of that for us!" I watched her beautiful, green eyes fill up with tears as she shared with me what Jesus had told her in Heaven and I started to cry. She shared this with such deep conviction and sadness. She couldn't believe he did this for us. I didn't have words to accurately respond to what she was telling me. I was just left there standing in our kitchen in shock. Hearing my three year old express such a powerful spiritual truth in such a simple, child-like manner was leaving me speechless.

She was teaching me about Jesus, when it should be the other way around. How is my three year old teaching me? I knew about Jesus dying for our sins … of course I knew that; but I guess in listening to her share she shared with such an awareness, it was personal to her now. What came across so vividly from Abigail in this moment was the passion and conflict her little heart was wrestling with; the reality for her was that it was all so sad that He has these "all better boo boos" but so good all at the same time. She was in a state of awe, wonder, and appreciation. I was learning and refreshing my view of our Savior and His sacrifice in these precious moments with my baby girl.

I thought to myself 'has life become so busy and ministry so redundant that we have lost the very meaning of why we even minister, why we are even saved?' He died a painful, gruesome death to give me freedom from my sin and He still bears the scars to this day to testify to that truth.

I learned a great deal that afternoon from my three year old. I learned the price He paid was greater than what I had previously considered. The truth of that old hymn took on a whole new meaning for me in that moment where it declares, "Jesus paid it all and all to him I owe…!"

After Abbey had described this interaction with Jesus she continued eating. Faith sat there with an upset look on her face.. I asked her what was wrong and she replied with a great amount of frustration, "I just don't like Abbey talking about heaven." I encouraged Faith to be supportive of Abbey and whatever she told her to just try her best to listen to her. Faith walked into the kitchen and put her plate away while Abbey pushed away from the kitchen table and went off to play.

Later that evening after Jason arrived home from work, I shared with him about what Abbey had told us about Jesus and His scars. He wasn't receiving it well and joyfully like I assumed he would. I asked him why he didn't seem to want to hear her talk about her time with Jesus in Heaven and he said it was because the more she would talk about heaven, the more reality repeatedly hit him that it all had really happened. I asked him to explain to me what he felt happened. He wouldn't answer me. I thought if he could just express what was in his heart and his thoughts that we could get past this silence and tension in our home surrounding what we all gone through.

As I was getting Abbey ready for bed that night she started jumping around and twirling. She jumped off our bed and started twirling and said with a big smile on her face, "This is what Jesus did with me, He twirled me round and round." I froze for a second and then said, "Abbey, show me what Jesus did with you." She twirled around and around the room and then she said, "He held my hand like this and he twirled me around like this mama!" I fell to my knees and cried until I could barely breathe. I grabbed Abbey and just held her close as I wept.

What flooded my heart and mind at that moment was while we were doing everything in our strength to bring her back to us here on earth, Jesus was immediately taking care of her in heaven. He was doing the things she loved to do like dancing with her and letting her do her twirls, walking around Heaven with her holding her little hand and laughing with her.

She shared with me how she felt so safe with him and that He was so much fun and so nice. I have no words that can adequately describe what my heart felt when I heard this. All I could do was cry (again) and thank Him for taking care of her when I could not. I am not a crier, my sister is the sensitive one, but I think I cried more tears every time Abbey talked about Heaven than I had in my whole life.. God was breaking me and teaching me with every word that came out of her mouth.

A mother's concern is that her children will always be taken care of. I never thought about Abbey being taken care of in heaven. I mean it's obvious she would be but to the level Jesus took care of her just humbled me. I couldn't get my mind off of the pictures in my head of Jesus twirling her around. I kept thinking about the scripture in Matthew 6:30 that says, *"Now if God so clothes the grass of the field, which today is, and tomorrow is thrown into the oven, will He not much more clothe you, O you of little faith?* He was doing just that with Abbey, He was taking care of her every need when we couldn't.

Abbey didn't feel any pain and had no clue that we were desperately working to get her heart to beat, she was in Heaven with Jesus, and was being cared for better than I could ever care for her. He created her and she was His daughter first. I was reminded that as much as I love her, He loves her more.

My love for Jesus has always been a part of me, but my daughter's stories about her time spent with Him were changing me. They were causing me to fall more and more in love with Jesus in a deeper way than I had previously known. I was seeing the Father side of God, the protector, and the friendship side of Him. I had always seen Him as holy and loving but I was realizing that there were so many facets to Him that I had not seen or experienced.

Later on that evening, Faith was getting ready for bed and she came out of the bathroom with a robe on. Abbey looked at her and said, "Oh, that's what Jesus wears!" A little confused, I asked, "A robe?" She answered very confidently, "Well yes and it was bluuuue (she said with lots of laughter)." I looked at Abbey and said, "A blue robe? Are you sure, honey?" She said, "Yes, I am sure it was blue and it had a gold thing right here" (she waved her hand across her chest). I asked her if she meant a sash and she just shrugged her shoulders. I don't think she understood what a sash was. I wasn't even sure why I asked that? I left it alone and stopped asking her anything further.

For a long time I didn't quite understand why Abbey saw Jesus in a robe that was blue. To be honest it was something that kind of left me perplexed because my image of Jesus was always in a white robe. I thought to myself maybe my image of Jesus was man made passed down from someone else's idea of what He looks like. Maybe how Abbey saw Jesus was different than how others saw Him? I had a lot of unanswered questions swirling around in my head. These questions would just have to be tucked away for now and hopefully later explained.

I laughed because it was just funny that these little things we were doing were causing her to be reminded of the things she saw in heaven. Faith just shrugged her shoulders and walked away.

Fast forward to me writing this book and I was writing the previous paragraph. I paused for a moment to think about her seeing Jesus in a blue robe. I just couldn't wrap my mind around

Jesus wearing a blue robe. I am aware that there are things we believe and are taught (like Christmas being in December) that aren't even found in scripture and it's very possible my image of Jesus wearing a white robe is one of those things. So I decided to dig a bit.

What I learned blew my mind. I was directed to Exodus 28 where it talks about how the robes were to be made for the High Priests. The entire chapter gives great detail as to how they were to be made. I did an internet search and found pictures artists have rendered to give an idea of what they would look like if we were to make one today and the main part of the priestly robe is....blue! Not only was the main part of the high priest's robe blue but the high priest's attire was also adorned with a golden breastplate across the chest. Abbey never said she saw a breastplate; she just quickly and flippantly said she saw a gold thing across His chest. The picture of what a high priest would have worn was actually very priestly in nature. It was beautifully adorned and looked nothing like the infamous white robe we were used to seeing in pictures. In fact I searched the Bible to try and find anywhere where it talks about Jesus wearing a white robe and I couldn't find a single scripture about it. In Matthew 17:2 it talks about Jesus being transfigured and His garments became white as the light. That is the only place in scripture where it talks about Jesus wearing a white garment. This was when he was on earth before he was crucified and resurrected. This was not a risen Jesus wearing a white robe.

I was left speechless! All these years later and her story is still revealing things to me.

Jesus is known to us as the High Priest in Hebrews 4:14, *"Therefore, since we have a great high priest who has ascended into heaven, Jesus the Son of God, let us hold firmly to the faith we profess."* So why would Abbey not see Him in priestly garments? I think it is entirely possible. I am not stating this as fact that Jesus wears garments a high priest would have worn but it is interesting to me that what Abbey described is what I found in scripture to be very similar to the priestly garments Exodus talks about.

When we were going to sleep that night, I asked Jason to tell me what he thought of everything she had said up until now. He just laid there silently in our bed for a few moments and then he said he was struggling with it all. He explained that he understood that scripture teaches us in 2 Cor. 5:8, as believers that "*To be absent from the body is to be present with the Lord*" but he was just struggling with the shock and reality of it all. He knew the biblically trained part, or we say, the religious part of him was also being challenged because he couldn't find fault in what she was saying with regard to scriptural accuracy. It was revealing to him and I just how much of dead and judgmental religion filled our hearts. We struggled with how this could be true. How could this be what she actually experienced? In all honesty what we were struggling with was really the fear of man and what others would think. Everything Abbey had shared was completely scriptural but in addition to that it was full of hope. We were learning that it didn't matter what people thought, it was beautiful what God did for her, and I wasn't going to allow the enemy to plant seeds of doubt in us. These thoughts were something we were battling in our minds but our hearts and our spirits said something different. They were telling us to listen to her and that's what we did.

    Jason wanted to hear everything she was sharing, but with every detail she told he was met with the reality that she really did die. He shared how he had to battle these tormenting thoughts like, "What if he did CPR wrong? What if he picked her up wrong?" It was all of the "what if's" that were constantly racing through his mind as he replayed that dreadful Saturday morning in his mind. Her dying meant she really was gone for those minutes when we were trying to resuscitate her. I was watching that reality set in in my husband, a reality that was causing these waves of emotions to wash over him repeatedly over the days and weeks ahead.

    I shared with him how I also struggled with everything that had happened and how it was a roller coaster of emotions we were on as a family. A traumatic event happened and then a wonderful miracle was given to our family. We watch our kids grow, and in the growing we watch them fall down and skin their knees. On some occasions they have to go get stitches but to watch your daughter pass away in your arms is a whole different level of emotions. What he had to watch and do for Abbey is not normal, it's not something you ever hope to experience. I reassured him that it's completely normal to feel shock, upset, or even grief over the incident we just went through. But God sent her back to us and she has this story to tell and even though it may be hard right now to hear, we have to steward it and allow it to be told. It's more than a story, it's a testimony of the power of God and it's meant to be shared.

I can feel it every time she shares something else about what she saw, heard or experienced. I reminded Jason that there is something greater than him and I at work here and God chose to deliver this testimony of His goodness through our little girl.

We agreed to let her share it when she remembered things but we wouldn't press her to share. We wanted her to have it come from her heart and in her time or God's time. We would allow this wonderful testimony of our baby girl being resurrected back to life, and the time she spent with Jesus, to be something that is born from her heart and not squeezed out of her memories.

8

Walking with Jesus

The next morning I was fixing the girls breakfast while Abbey and Faith were playing dress up in the other room. Faith came running into the kitchen very upset saying, "Mama, Abbey is talking about Heaven again and I don't like it!" I knelt down next to her and said, "Why does it bother you so much, Faith?" Faith paused for a second with her arms folded in disagreement and a frown on her face and then she said, "Because if she went to Heaven that means that she died and she didn't die because she is here with us now." I held Faith close to me while she cried her little eyes out. This was the first time she had really talked about how she felt since Abbey's accident.

"I understand what you are saying honey but when Abbey had her accident she went to be with Jesus for a short time while we were trying to get her to come back to us. I know it's hard for your little heart to understand but Jesus took good care of her while she was with Him. You and your sisters prayed for her to come back and to be healed and God answered your prayers. What matters is that she is here with us now and she is perfectly fine. I know it's hard to hear her talk about Heaven but we have to let her tell her story. When she shares with you her stories about Heaven instead of getting upset, how about you just pray and thank Jesus for healing Abbey and sending her back to us?"

I prayed with Faith and gave her a big hug. She said she would work hard to not get upset but she just loved Abbey and she never wanted to lose her. After we finished our talk Faith ran to play with her little sister. Faith and Abbey are best friends, they have been ever since Abbey could walk. Whether it's making a waterslide out of their small play slide in their bedroom in the dead of winter, or deciding to build a snowman in the middle of the kitchen floor- they have always been two peas in a pod, getting into mischief together. Usually the ideas are all Faith's and Abbey just goes along with whatever Faith says. Abbey thinks the sun rises and sets with Faith. While Abbey's accident was hard for us all to process, it seemed especially hard for Faith's heart to understand everything at just five years old. Faith was and always has been there to protect Abbey in a big sister kind of a way, so I think she struggled with her accident because she wasn't able to protect her that time.

We were on the way to pick up Hannah and Lizzie from school later that day in the car when Abbey said to me, "Mama, did you know Heaven is bright?" I glanced at her in the rear view mirror and said, "I did not, what colors are in heaven?" Abbey responded with, "All kinds, Mommy, Heaven is beautiful." I have no idea what caused her to remember that unless it was just staring out the car window at the sunshine or maybe she saw some pretty flowers in the distance. Usually whenever she talks about Heaven or Jesus it is because something she saw caused her to remember.

She shared with me how Jesus held her hand and walked with her and showed her different places in heaven. She told me how He was just so nice and how He laughed and laughed with her. My eyes welled up with tears yet again while she was telling me these things about Him.

Every time she talked about Jesus I just felt the presence of God so strong in everything she was saying. There was no denying this happened just by the way she expressed her time spent in Heaven … especially her time spent with Jesus. Before Abbey's accident she spoke nonstop about her favorite ice princess. Now that storybook character had taken a back seat to her new friend, Jesus. He was all she could talk about and I loved watching that part of this journey unfold.

I have served Him most of my life and I have never needed a reason to love Him. He has always been part of my life and the times when I felt He wasn't near, when I look back on my life, were the times when He was actually the nearest. What He did for me on the cross has always been enough for me but there was a short season of four years where I thought it wasn't enough.

When I was seventeen years old, while still a young girl in many ways, I was hurting and I was carrying around this huge weight of grief that I didn't really know how to deal with. I didn't know how to be free from the sadness and brokenness I lived with. I had become bitter and I had many walls I had perfectly built up around my heart, while still wearing a big smile on my face, so that no one really knew.

I remember arguing with my dad in our kitchen one morning about whether God even existed and I argued that I especially didn't believe that the Holy Spirit was real anymore. I said "if He is real and all of this is true, where is He? Where is the Holy Spirit for our family? He is supposed to be our Comforter but I don't feel Him. We lost Matthew (my brother) to suicide after three years of contending through prayer and fasting and now we are left with shattered hearts and the ashes of what used to be our family unit. If God exists where did He go?! He has forgotten about us! I don't feel God or His Spirit. The only thing I feel is darkness and all I see are traces of what we used to be." My dad had tears well up in his eyes and He just looked at me and said, "Honey, He has been carrying us every second since Matthew left us, it's the enemy who wants you to believe otherwise." I could tell it was reopening a very familiar wound in my dad's heart so I stopped talking about it and ran out the back kitchen door to school.

That night I couldn't sleep so I got up and read my Bible for the first time in years and when I opened it up, my eyes fell upon the scripture from Isaiah 61:1-3. For the first time in years I heard the Lord speak to me and He said, "This is my promise to you and your family, Sarah. I will heal your broken hearts, I will comfort you, I will exchange your ashes for beauty, I will give you my oil of joy for your mourning, if you allow me to." I remember weeping more that night in my bedroom than I ever had before. I had learned how to live with this lump in my throat called grief. I had learned to smile instead of cry when people would bring up my brother. I put all pictures and conversations about my brother and his death away in fear that it would continue to bring pain to my parents. All this did was delay the grief process in my life which resulted in pain, bitterness, and this big canyon between me and my relationship with God.

I prayed that night and said, "God, if You are real and You really do care about us and haven't forgotten about our family then I need You to remove this hurt. I need You to reach down deep into my heart and I need You to take it all away at once. I can't handle going through the process of healing any longer, either remove it all or don't remove any of it.

A week later my dad had convinced me to go to a church service. It was a larger church in our area where an evangelist and his wife had been ministering. It was a Friday night and I went out of respect for my dad. The evangelist's wife, Kathy, had ministered that night. She spoke on how she was filled with hatred and anger and she had been living with it for so long she didn't even realize it was there. She shared how it had affected almost every relationship in her life and how she wouldn't let anyone in because of it. God had set her free and every single relationship was drastically changed and restored. I was a teenage girl who had come to this service with so much hurt on the inside and a mountain of grief. I stood in that crowd like a needle in a haystack that night. I related very much to the message and felt as though she was preaching straight to me that evening. I knew I wanted to be free, I just didn't know how.

At the altar call she walked down off that stage and made her way through the crowd right down to me. She put her hand on my head and prayed a word of knowledge over me that she could not have possibly known. She "read my mail" prophetically by the power of the Holy Spirit and instantly I felt all the anger and hurt that grief had left me with leave and in return I immediately was filled with the Holy Spirit. Something left and in its place something was given to me. God did exactly what He promised me He would do just a week earlier. The exchange that took place was my ashes, all the broken pieces of my life and heart and he gave me beauty instead.

I left that night feeling ten times lighter and the smile that was on my face was real for the first time since my brother, who I loved dearly, had died.

I share this story to tell of how God has been faithful to me. This is one of many reasons I serve Him. His cross is enough but He didn't stop at the cross. The sacrifice He made for us all on the cross was only the beginning for us. He is very much a God who is near to the brokenhearted and He longs to have a relationship with us. He calls us into a relationship that is not based on religion but on His love for us. I follow His word because I want to; because I know its protection for me. My relationship with Him is what gives me life.

Every word my little girl shared about Jesus changed and challenged my heart afresh. Life had caused me to allow some religious minded roots to grow in areas of my heart. Abigail's testimony was challenging me to return to the seventeen year old me that was rescued from one of the deepest darkest valleys I had ever been in. I needed to return to that place of total abandonment and complete trust in my relationship with God and as my daughter shared that is exactly what was happening. This journey we were on was exposing that there was so much unbelief in my heart. How could I have gotten so off track from where God had restored me and healed me? I didn't even realize I was off track until I started analyzing everything Abbey would share.

I remember falling to my knees in my bedroom later thanking Him over and over again for sending her back to us. I repented for my unbelief and for allowing a religious spirit to take root in my heart. I asked Him to remove it all…once again in my life. I prayed that very familiar prayer that I had prayed so many years ago. I expressed to Jesus how I knew this was a gift to our family and I was so humbled that He would have mercy on us and give her back to us. This response I had is one that you will read over and over again in this book … but it's true.

We were rushing to get out the door a few days later to pick up my older two daughters from school and Abbey stopped me and said, "Mama, I want you to show me a picture of Jesus on the cross." I responded with, "Honey, we have to go get your sisters right now we don't have time." Abbey just looked at me with a look of longing in her eyes, "Mama, I want to see one right now, please."

"I don't think you will like seeing these pictures because it will hurt your heart, Jesus isn't on the cross anymore you know that, you walked with him in heaven."

"Mama, PLEASE I just want to see a picture on your phone." So with reluctance I did an internet search of pictures of Jesus on the cross and pulled some up. Abbey clicked on one and with her little fingers she zoomed in on a picture of Jesus on the cross and her eyes welled up with tears. "Mama, this is what He did for us. He did this for our sins."

We drove off to get my girls and I glanced in the rear view mirror at Abbey as she stared out the window deep in thought. Tears trickled down my face as I thought to myself, *"What happened to her in heaven?"* What did she see or experience that would cause her three year old self to go from a "Jesus lives in my heart understanding" to a broken "Jesus did this for our sins" level of revelation?

I realized right then that my little girl was never going to be the same. She was a different little girl than from before her accident. She no longer talked about her favorite movie or sang her favorite song at the top of her lungs from that soundtrack that she loved so much. She talked about Jesus. He was her obsession. Not even Heaven was her focus, Jesus was front of mind and heart with Abbey and I was an absolute mess concerning it all.

Here I am, her mother, the one who is supposed to teach her about Jesus and she was teaching *me*. My sweet little Abigail Joy-whose name means "Joy of the Father"-was a completely different little girl. At three years old, she was broken and had an understanding of Jesus and His sacrifice for our sins, that to be honest ... I didn't even possess.

I had always been taught, no matter what you read or how much ministry training you receive, that brokenness is not something you obtain, it's something that is thrust upon you through adversity.

Brokenness was something that was all too familiar to me because of what my family and I walked through with the death of my brother. I can recognize when someone has become broken before the Lord from a mile away. Abbey was broken. What does that mean? It's hard to put words to it, it just means through various trials or experiences that you didn't ask to go through; your understanding of who Jesus is becomes deeper, and more intimate. It's when you get up from those trials and you walk with a limp forever just like Jacob in the Old Testament did after he wrestled with God all through the night, leaving his encounter with Yahweh with a permanent sign of his brokenness from the encounter. It's something many pray for but few experience.

When I attended ministry school I would hear many students pray and cry out for God to make them broken and I would just shake my head and say to myself, *"You don't know what you are asking for."* Brokenness is not some notch on your ministry belt; it's far more precious than that. It is sacred…It is holy.

9

Two Crosses

Sunday had finally come for Abbey and she was so excited to finally start her new class at church. It had been a week since Abbey's accident and what a week it was! Our family had begun to get used to hearing Abbey share all her stories about going to Heaven and it wasn't as much of a shock to hear anymore. Our girls were so sweet to her and would listen intently, allowing her to have that safe space with them. I know at the time they didn't fully understand everything she was sharing but they never let her feel like they didn't. Her stories were always welcome with them and I am so thankful for that.

I am pretty sure there are so many things Jason and I never heard because she would share with her sisters. Some would get retold to us but I am sure some didn't and I am ok with that. I think it makes it even more special, a sister thing.

God himself only knows how many stories were told to Faith. Faith can be summed up like this; she is our wild mustang who loves Jesus, her family, and people with her whole heart and then some. But she marches to the beat of her own drum. I can promise Abbey probably shared an entire book of stories with Faith about Jesus and her time with Him and who knows if we will ever hear them. Faith and Abbey have an unshakeable bond even to this day. Their relationship is a rare and special one.

On that Sunday morning we all piled into our car and went to church. Jason and I were the youth pastors at our church at the time, so naturally the pastoral staff all knew what happened to Abbey and they had been praying for her since the accident took place. I shared with our children's pastor what Abbey had told us about going to Heaven because I wanted her to be aware in case she started to share things in class. Our children's pastor was so understanding and she is just a wonderful woman of God so I knew she would do everything she could to make Abbey feel safe. In fact she is one of our dearest friends and still in ministry alongside us to this day.

Abbey was so excited to go to church because it was going to be her first official day in her preschool class, *Little Sparks*. She had been asking to go in there for almost a year because she felt like the nursery was too babyish for her. Abbey was very advanced for her age, she talked from an early age and had the vocabulary and understanding of a kindergartener, probably because she had three older sisters she was trying to keep up with.

We dropped her off at her class and as I glanced back I saw her infamous Abbey smile light up her face and I couldn't help but smile as well. She made it there, it may have been a week late but she was there and she was safe. I had many of these moments in the weeks and months after her accident. Many thoughts of how close we came to losing her, many moments that took my breath away, and many times of thankfulness.

After church when I picked her up from class, her teacher pulled me aside and explained to me how Abbey had shared some interesting things. Immediately my stomach dropped, "Oh no, I thought…what is she going to tell me?" Abbey sharing about

Heaven had become something we were getting used to as a family but that doesn't necessarily mean it was normal to others.

I could feel my mama bear rising up inside of me, and my face felt as though it was on fire. I answered her with a lump in my throat, "Oh she did…what did she say?" At this point I could feel myself starting to sweat profusely. Her teacher responded with, "After we did our lesson today, Abbey started to tell us that she went to Heaven and met Jesus. She drew on her paper two crosses not three and said she met the man on the other cross and his name was Joseph. I just thought you would want to know that." The teacher had a smile on her face and said it so nonchalantly.

I responded with, "Yes, she did share that with me and I am sure there will be more stories to come. Thank you for allowing her to share, we are just taking this one day at a time." I didn't want to apologize because how could I set that kind of example to my daughter? There was nothing to apologize for, she had done nothing wrong. I knew this was all probably overwhelming for a teacher to process but if it was then this teacher never let on that it was a problem.

Abbey had shared with me a few days earlier about meeting the thief on the cross in heaven. She did not describe him as a thief but for reference I am.

"Mama did you know that there was a man who died on the cross next to Jesus?" I said to her, "Yes but actually honey, there were two men who died next to Jesus." She responded with a confused look on her face, "Umm nope there was only one man and he was on a cross too next to Jesus. I met him, mama and his name is Joseph and he is so nice." I was a little puzzled at first on how to explain to her so she could understand. I knew the reason she didn't meet the other one was because he wasn't there but I was trying to help her understand there were two men who hung on the cross next to Jesus. I wanted her to know one denied him while one saw Jesus for who He was, his savior. I explained to her the best way I could, "Actually honey there were two men who were thieves that hung on the cross next to Jesus, one accepted Jesus and one mocked

Him. She looked at me and said "there was? Welllllll, I met Joseph and he is sooo nice.

All her heart and mind could process at the time was that she met a man named Joseph and he died next to Jesus, nothing more was told to her about this story while she was in heaven. Abbey didn't refer to him as a thief like we do. She just said he died on the cross next to Jesus.

Later when I was thinking about her description of him I realized that in Heaven we are not known for the sinful things we did, we are new creations, all old things (sin) have passed away and are made new. This is why she didn't understand me when I tried to explain who he was in the bible. Why would Jesus refer to him as a thief to Abbey when he was a new man? He didn't! Jesus simply introduced him as Joseph and to Abbey he wasn't a thief he was a nice man she met.

I knew right away why she didn't meet two men and why she only met one man. Scripture clearly states one man believed He was the Son of God and one didn't. Abbey calling him a man named Joseph and not a thief is what had me at a loss for words. My eyes filled with tears as I thought about God's love for us, it's a love that surpasses all of our understanding, it's a love we have been conditioned by the world to reject, it's a love that is so costly yet free for those who choose to receive it. I was reminded of the passage of scripture in *Psalms 103:10-13* where David says, *"He has not dealt with us according to our sins. Nor punished us according to our iniquities. For as the heavens are high above the earth, So great is His mercy toward those who fear Him; As far as the east is from the west, so far has He removed our transgressions from us."*

God sees us for who we were meant to be, who He created us to be ... not who we were when we were in our sin. Jesus saw the thief on the cross's belief and his repentance and that was enough for him. His past was no longer a part of him, it was instantly forgotten. How beautiful is the redeeming power of God.

What blows my mind is, here is a man full of sin being crucified on the cross, he even willingly admitted he was guilty and deserved this death sentence that he was enduring all while hanging next to the sinless One who is literally dying right then for this man's sin. Wow! The very essence of this story blows me away. He is literally forgiving a man while dying for the right for this man to be forgiven. Jesus the perfect lamb who was slain for this thief and for all who accept and surrender to His great love. Jesus gave us the example of the new covenant by His interaction with the thief on the cross. This thief on the cross's new heart and his repentance bypassed all his sin and all the Father saw was him made anew. Wow!

This is why I say my religious barriers were being ripped away with every word Abbey shared. In my heart God was peeling back layers of unbelief that I didn't realize were even there. Yes, unbelief! I was realizing yet again that I had put God in this religious box that I referred to as Christianity. I could only believe in what my mind would allow me to. Anything that didn't require "work" just wasn't God. Anything that sounded or looked weird just wasn't God. I had packaged Him in a pretty little religious box and this box was being blown into a million pieces. I found myself seemingly not in control anymore and I loved it.

He is holy and I believe in holiness because I don't believe in giving God my left overs. I believe He is worthy of my best. That's not what I am talking about here, what I am saying is that if it didn't fit the small space in my religious mindset then it wasn't God. Don't get me wrong I am a fireball and I absolutely love the Holy Spirit. I love to see God move and I have lived my life in search of more of Him. What I mean is somehow without even knowing it I had allowed this unbelief even though it was small to be rooted in my heart.

We believe in some pretty interesting things as believers, Jesus being born of a virgin, Jesus dying on the cross and being raised from the dead three days later, God forming man out of dust, Noah's Ark, a man being swallowed by a whale, Ezekiel lying on his side for over a year as a demonstration to the people of Israel, etc. I can read the Bible and believe everything it says as truth but I couldn't believe my daughter telling me that when she died she was with Jesus. I realized that I had a religious spirit that I needed

Jesus to set me free from. I desperately needed to see Jesus from the eyes of this thief who hung on the cross next to Him and simply believed. I needed my belief to be born from a desperate need of the Father's love and I needed to be reminded of what He saved me from, my own shortcomings and sinful ways.

I think when you live life and especially when you do ministry somewhere along the way you can become a little hardened. You can allow the disappointments of life to leave behind a souvenir in your heart and spirit. The effects of this are unfortunately some not so pretty things you find are inside of you, like a measure of unbelief.

As I am writing this chapter I am listening to a song about being His beloved and the words go something like this, "I am your beloved you have bought me with your blood, and on your hand you have written out my name, I am your beloved the one the Father loves, mercy has defeated all my shame." This song resonates with me on so many levels. This is exactly what God was beginning to do in my heart seven years ago through the testimony of my beautiful Abigail. I found myself wanting nothing except all of Jesus and everything He had for me even if my mind didn't understand it. I was so undone and I just knew that there was a desperation for more brewing with every moment I listened to Abbey share.

I couldn't help but think of Jesus introducing this man to Abbey and how He could have also introduced the other thief if he would have simply believed. How humbling that a man who lived a life of sin hung next to Jesus and when presented with the truth of who Jesus was he immediately surrendered his heart. Right then his former life and ways were erased and he was a new man in the sight of the Lamb of God. *"Behold! The Lamb of God who takes away the sin of the world!" John 1:29.* He could do nothing to earn God's love; he was out of time yet the posture of his heart to ask the Son of God to remember him was enough. We serve a holy God and we also serve a loving and just God.

I was a little nervous to share about Abbey meeting the man on the cross because his name is not mentioned in scripture and we always want to keep this story aligned with scripture. It doesn't go against scripture, his name just isn't mentioned. Obviously there are going to be things she shares that aren't necessarily in scripture but it doesn't mean they go against scripture either.

For example, her dancing with Jesus isn't in scripture but I believe it is in line with the character of Jesus. In Matthew 19:13 scripture says, *"Let the little children come to Me, and do not forbid them; for of such is the kingdom of heaven."* Jesus loves children and He never turned them away and He still doesn't.

On our way home from church, I shared with Jason how she drew only two crosses on her coloring page and how she informed her teacher that she had met Joseph, the man on the cross. These are conversations I never would have dreamed of having with my husband about one of our children and yet here we were. This was our life now.

I would constantly have questions go through my mind such as, "Is what she is saying real?" to which I would answer my own thoughts, "Of course this is real how else would my three year old have such a mature understanding of Jesus? How would she know some of the things she was sharing with us?"

We were parents who were raising our kids to know and love God but we also were parents who believed in slowly maturing them in the things of the Lord. We wanted them to be children while they were children. We believed every stage of a child's life both physically and spiritually are necessary and they should not be rushed to grow up. God would naturally grow our kids to reflect Him more and more as they grew. We would sing children's church songs and I would tell them who Jesus was and that He lived in their heart and that He was born in a manger in Bethlehem, very basic children's stories but nothing really beyond that.

This is a large part of how I knew she experienced what she did, because Abbey's knowledge was wise beyond her years after spending time with Jesus in heaven. It wasn't that she had an adult understanding, it was that she had a Heaven understanding. Her understanding was different, it was pure and hadn't been tainted by the world. It was an understanding I didn't even have in my many years of serving Him.

10

Flip Flops

Over the next several weeks there were many more stories Abbey would share with us, her friends, and her teachers at children's church. Jason and I had agreed, when her accident first happened and Abbey had begun to share about her time spent in Heaven with Jesus, that we would let her tell us on her own and in her own time. We thought it would be better to not prod her or ask her a million questions, but just let her tell it when she needed to. We would do our best to provide a safe space for her to share. We would ask a few questions here and there but usually only when she would start sharing. Her beautiful story stayed true and pure because of this.

As the weeks went by our initial shock of that dreadful day in September had worn off. We had become more used to Abbey sharing with us and others about Heaven and Jesus. She shared with everyone she could, and at the most random times and places. We would be in the grocery store standing in line and she would blurt out to a complete stranger, "Did you know Jesus is real and I met him?" We would be volunteering in the lunchroom at her sister's school and I would sit Abbey right next to me and while I was working I would hear her telling one of the students there about heaven. She shared with neighborhood kids and their moms, which didn't always go over well. She would share with kids on her sports team. It didn't matter where she was or to whom, she would just start sharing.

As a mom I had to get used to this and allow the worry of man's opinion of us to be ripped off of me like a band-aid. About two years after Abbey's accident at around five years old, she was sharing with some friends of hers that were very close to our family. They responded to her with some not so nice opinions about her story. They accused her of making it all up to get attention. They said a lot of hurtful things that honestly floored me since it was coming from people who were supposed to love her. She came to me crying her eyes out after this happened. I will never forget what she said to me, "Mama, how can someone believe that Heaven is real and that Heaven is where we go to when we die but not believe I went when I died?" She couldn't understand how or why they would think she could make it all up. She even asked me if I believed her. My heart was broken at the sight of my little girl's heart being broken. Words hurt and they are powerful, and I found myself wanting to keep this from ever happening again. I began to think we need to just keep this to ourselves and keep Abbey from being ridiculed. I knew these thoughts were wrong and faithless.

It was the first time Abbey experienced resistance to her experience. I think it hurt her so deeply because it came from people she was very close to. Up to this moment everyone so far had believed her and was so blessed by her testimony. If someone didn't believe her then they never told her, and they just kept it to themselves.

I tried my best to explain to her that there will be people who don't believe her and there will also be people in her lifetime who don't believe in Jesus regardless of her experience. This was such a hard conversation to have because her faith was so big. Her heart was broken and she was hurt and there wasn't much I could do to fix this.

I explained to her that this assignment Jesus gave her was going to come with a whole lot more resistance, that there would be more kids and adults who would say what she experienced didn't happen. I told her this journey would be hard but she was strong enough to do it and we would be right there to help her.

I encouraged her to tell her story anyway and to remember who sent her back to us and what He told her to do. I explained to her the countless lives she would touch would far outweigh the ones who criticized. Abbey had a story to tell and the world needed to hear it.

We shared her story whenever we had the opportunity to, per our Abigail's request. Jason shared it to strangers on airplanes and with friends. We shared it with family members, her Grandparents shared it with neighbors and complete strangers. Her Papaw shared it at a men's breakfast. Jason's pastor from his hometown shared it with so many as well because it had such an impact on his own life. Her story was spreading and being told to so many who were in need of hope. We would receive emails and phone calls telling us how thankful they were to hear it and how much it impacted them.

My family, who knows me well, always accuses me of being very private. I don't like to share my private life at all. I'll share a few pics here and there on social media but that is it. I keep the intimate details of our life to a very select few.

Abbey, however, was stretching me in this area. All sense of us keeping this story to a few friends and our family was being blown out of the water. Isn't that what kids do though? We have our ways of doing things all packaged up neatly and kids come along and mess them up (in a good way). It teaches us humility and to not bow to the crippling opinion of man. I love kids and I love the way they live fearlessly, without any care to what people think of them. My daughter could wear flower shorts with a striped shirt and rain boots all with a great big sense of pride on her face. I absolutely love this about children, their innocent way of looking at life humbles me and brings me back to the childlike faith I once had.

Jason's faith was also growing like mine, or should I say it was being restored. The layers that life's disappointments had built up around our hearts was slowly being peeled back one by one and the deeper faith Jesus had called us to was being revealed and growing more and more. His upset he had surrounding her accident was being replaced with gratefulness and peace. He was realizing that although we knew we came close to losing her, what we received back was indeed a gift. It took a minute to get there but we were getting there.

We were hanging out with our kids one day when Abbey curled up in my lap and said to me, "Mama, can you show me a picture of Jesus on your phone again?" I pulled up a picture of Jesus on the cross just as I had several times already when she would ask. As I explained in previous chapters, Abbey would get emotional every time she saw the picture of Jesus on the cross but then she would say with the greatest conviction, "Jesus did this for us Mama." I asked Jason on this day when she asked us again to pull up a picture, why he thought she wanted to see Him on the cross specifically. Jason had a pretty good revelation about it.

Jason explained to me that while he was preparing to preach the Sunday morning service at our church God gave him a revelation about this. While he was praying over the message, he asked the Lord a simple question … "Lord, why is my little girl so obsessed with you being on the cross?" The answer Jason received was sudden and straightforward; he heard the Holy Spirit's voice whisper to his heart, "Jason, Abbey is obsessed with my sacrifice on the cross because all of Heaven has been and will always be obsessed with the cross throughout all of eternity they have sung and will sing, 'Worthy is the Lamb who was slain.'"

It was so true and it pierced right through all of the remaining feelings that Jason had been trying to navigate through. Abbey came back from Heaven focused on what Heaven is focused on - the Lamb who was slain and who will forever be worthy of all honor, glory, wisdom, power and might. She was reflecting on earth the passion for Jesus' sacrifice that she had encountered in Heaven - plain and simple.

As I pulled up a picture of Jesus on the cross she said to me, "No, no, mama I just want to see a picture of Jesus." I was surprised and I quickly did an internet search of pictures of Jesus. When I pulled up the hundreds of people's attempt at painting or drawing a picture of Jesus I told her these aren't actually Jesus, these are just people's ideas of what they think He looked like. She quickly zoomed in on a picture of Jesus with shorter hair and she said, "That's Jesus!" "That's Him mama!"

She went on to describe His eyes as being a blue like color. She wasn't set on calling them just blue like a lot of our family members' eyes are. She was trying her best to describe this blue in her little three year old language but the best she could do was to say, "His eyes are a really pretty blue color but different."

She said he had a beard like her daddy's but all over his face. At the time Jason had a goatee beard. I sat there thinking about this picture she pointed out to me. It happened to be a picture that a little girl painted when she was a little older than Abbey. It had become a famous picture and to be honest I was surprised Abbey said it looked like Jesus. The image in my mind of what I thought Jesus might look like was not like this picture that Abbey was showing me. This Jesus had short hair and a short beard which was very different from the Jesus image I had remembered from my Sunday school days.

I realized right then that we as Christains get so tripped up with details like these that we can literally miss Him altogether just as the Pharisees did. It doesn't matter if Jesus had short hair or long hair, a long beard or short beard, blue eyes, green eyes, or fiery eyes, just as long as we don't miss Him.

It was around a few weeks later when we were shopping in a store, we passed by an aisle where they had some flip flops for sale. Abbey stopped at these sandals and said, "Mama, Jesus wears flip flops." I kind of paused for a second and with my head slightly tilted and in disbelief I said, "Jesus wears flip flops like you? Do you think maybe you saw sandals on his feet and you think they are flip flops?" Abbey responded so sure of herself, "Nope, He wears flip flops like mine but a little different." When I asked her what she meant by different she quickly said like hers but there was stuff right here and she swooped her little hands across her ankles. I instantly thought in mind that she saw sandals but she was calling them flip flops because to her sandals are flip flops. I did however continue to wrestle with that part of her story but shrugged it off until I was writing this book and knew I had to include it. I stopped writing for a while because I didn't want to put this part in the story only for her to be ridiculed once again but I knew I couldn't hold back pieces in the name of ridicule.

One day I decided to push through it and write it but while I was typing I heard the Lord say, "Ask me for wisdom." I did and I suddenly had this idea to do an internet search for sandals that may have been excavated from the time Jesus walked the earth. I wanted to see if by chance there have been some sandals found during excavations in Israel. What I found was that there were sandals found in a cave next to the cave the Dead Sea scrolls were discovered in. These sandals are actually on display in the same museum as the Dead Sea scrolls. They are described to be sandals that would have been worn in Jesus's day.

Someone rendered a drawing of what these sandals would look like restored to their original condition since they were old and somewhat decayed. I didn't need the picture because I could see what they looked like even through the decay on the picture of the original sandals. My eyes filled with tears as I couldn't believe what I was seeing. These sandals looked like leather flip flops with a strap around the ankle that you would tie. I reached for my Bible and read the scripture in *John 1:27 "It is He who comes after me, of whom I am not worthy even to untie the strap of His sandal."* While reading this passage I could envision what John the Baptist meant by not being worthy to even untie his sandals. This simple little treasure meant so much to me as a mom. I couldn't wrap my mind around

Jesus wearing flip flops and this picture showed me exactly what I believe Abbey saw in heaven. What I needed was just to think like a child, very simply.

All these years later and the Lord was still revealing truths from her time spent in heaven.

Abbey shared with us a few days later how beautiful Heaven was. She told me that Heaven was not only bright and full of colors but that there was always singing. She shared how she loved all the singing and how beautiful it sounded. I asked her what songs they sang in Heaven and she said she didn't know the songs but she just remembered that the singing was so pretty.

She continued to share that day more about heaven. She said to me, "Mama, Jesus walked with me all over and He showed me so many things. Did you know there is a river in Heaven and trees?" I just answered like I always did, "Oh really that is wonderful, Abbey." She continued on explaining to me that the river and trees He showed her were special. She said Jesus pointed them out to her and said, "That river and those trees are special and they mean something." She didn't ever tell me what they meant but just that Jesus took her near them so she could see them.

She went on to tell me how special she felt in Heaven and how safe she was. She explained that Jesus made her feel safe and so loved. Something a mama's heart needed to hear. While we were trying to get her heart beating again and trying to breathe life back into her lungs in the midst of our chaos, panic and pain, He was taking good care of her in heaven. He was making her feel safe and loved and showing her all of these beautiful and meaningful things in heaven.

When she was sharing about this beautiful river she saw and these tree's Jesus showed her, I knew that in Revelation it talks about a river and a tree of life. I searched scriptures and found this passage in *Revelation 22:1-2*, *"And he showed me a pure river of water of life, clear as crystal, proceeding from the throne of God and of the Lamb. In the middle of its street, and on either side of the river, was the tree of life, which bore twelve fruits, each tree yielding its fruit every month."*

I couldn't help but think about whether this river and trees were what John saw or could they be what the Psalmist was referring to in *Psalms 46:4a, "There is a river whose streams shall make glad the city of our God."* The river of life gives life and I find it so fitting that He walked by it and pointed it out to my little girl, the one who in the natural world was fighting for her own life. The giver of life was holding her little hand and with each step He took with her He was filling her up with the knowledge of who He was. Heaven was making an imprint, not only on her heart and mind, but in her spirit as well. Abbey was receiving more than just her earthly life back; she was being filled up with heaven's heartbeat.

Abbey would never be able to see Jesus the same as she did before her accident. I found myself wanting the same experience. I didn't want to die but I found myself longing to see Jesus, to hold His hand, to have Him strip away all of the layers of worry, doubt, and fear the world had put on me. I wanted His mindset, I wanted His heart, I wanted to emulate Heaven not be weighed down by the burdens of this world. I found myself wanting more and more of Him. That's what Abbey's description of Jesus and Heaven did for me. It caused me to be dissatisfied with religion and to long for a deeper relationship with my Creator. I found myself imagining lying at the feet of Jesus with his nail pierced "all better boo boo's" and his leather "flip flops" and worshiping Him in all His glory. I found myself wanting to twirl round and round with Him, to be child-like in my faith again.

11

Bonnie Jean

A few weeks after Abigail's accident my husband, Jason had received a job transfer to Atlanta, Ga. where he was asked to take on a new role within his company. We had felt a year earlier that God was preparing to move us on, so when this came we were not surprised in the least. We were so sure we were being moved on we had even shared with our pastor to start looking to replace us as youth pastors. We had spent almost seven years in Colorado and made so many lasting relationships but it was time to move into the next chapter the Lord had for us. It was hard to leave but we obeyed God's leading, and the doors He had opened and we moved on.

We made the journey towards the east coast with our little family to begin our new chapter in Georgia. With Colorado in the rear view mirror and some very sad little girls we tried our best to settle into our new home.

My birthday was the month we moved to Georgia and I had received a package from my sister shortly after we settled in. She had given me a framed picture of our Grandparents from our dad's side. It was a photo that our grandmother had kept on her bedside table in her room. They had both passed on and with Jesus now, but they left such an imprint on all of our lives. I missed them terribly. My sister and my parents were the only ones who had a picture of them in their homes. I had often said to my sister how I wanted to make a copy of the one she had and put it on display in my house. The picture was of them in their early thirties, they were young, vibrant, and full of life. I never had the chance to make a copy before we moved. My sister not only gave me a picture of them but it was the original one my grandmother proudly had on display in her home. To receive this brought such comfort to my heart in the midst of extreme homesickness.

We had the most wonderful Grandparents; they were God fearing, loving and so kind. My grandmother, whose name was Bonnie Jean is probably the one who I can point to in my life who had the greatest influence on me spiritually. She was a wonderful woman who was known for her strength and the authority she carried. She would pray and demons would scatter. She carried a mantle on her that we all felt and missed terribly. She had a way of making you feel like you were the most important person in the room. She would light up a room when she walked in and her smile and hugs would bring peace to any upset you may have been feeling. Her presence alone and who she was in the Lord commanded a room. The atmosphere would shift when she would enter a place. My grandfather had the sweetest spirit and was so full of joy and kindness, he would smile at you and you knew everything was fine. He loved Jesus so much and his life showed that. Even though my Grandpa was a wonderful man I spent a lot more time with my Grandma. My mom gave me this gift; she gladly stepped out of the way and allowed her mother-in-law to influence us and to spend a great deal of time with us. She did it all without a hint of jealousy. I am forever grateful to my mother for this. I know this is not always the case when it comes to in laws. Unfortunately none of our children were able to meet my Grandma and only my oldest met my Grandpa as a baby. They passed away before they were born or old enough to form a relationship with them. This was something we all grieved because they were some of the most wonderful people we all had the privilege of knowing.

I unpackaged the picture and put it on display on an end table in our formal living room with great pride in my heart. A few weeks had gone by and Abbey and Faith were running and chasing each other around the house. Abbey came running into the living room where I was sitting and she brought the picture of my Grandparents with her and she said to me, "Mama, who is this as she pointed to my grandmother in the picture?" I replied, "Honey, that's my Grandma but you never were able to meet her because she went to Heaven before you were born." Abbey responded with her sweet voice, "I met her in Heaven and she chased me around tickling me." Before I could even stop Abbey to ask a million questions she ran off to play.

I sat there for a moment thinking about what she had just shared. Just a few months previously, when her accident first happened, I had asked Abbey if she saw or met my grandmother in heaven. I didn't have many loved ones in Heaven but my grandmother was one that I named off of my list to see if Abbey had possibly met her. It was one of the few questions I had asked her and her response at the time was, "My Grandma is in heaven?" She thought I was telling her my mom, her Grandma, was in Heaven and she panicked at first thinking her Grandma had died. She was very confused and she was getting upset by me asking her so I just didn't even pursue the subject again.

My grandmother was such a huge influence in my life and a huge prayer warrior for us. I remember being a teenager and hearing my grandmother up praying through the night for my future children and husband. I was one of the closest grandkids to my Grandma because she lived so close to us. I would sit at her feet and listen to all her great ministry stories growing up and would always think about how blessed I was to have the best Grandma in the world. I am pretty sure I was her favorite…if I can say that without my siblings or cousins getting too upset with me. Of course I am sure they would say the same. That is how my grandmother made you feel, like you were her favorite. I thought if my grandmother knew her great grandchild, someone who she had prayed for long before Abbey was even born, her Sarah Sue's baby girl, was there in Heaven even for a moment she would beg Jesus to let her meet her. My Grandma was not someone you could say no to easily, her compassionate heart, blue eyes and warm smile would cause you to give her anything she wanted.

As I sat there and pondered what Abbey had said, I quickly dismissed the reality of this happening. I thought to myself, she just isn't remembering correctly because this was the first time I had heard this and secondly I don't remember my grandmother ever tickling or chasing any of us kids. Although I really wanted this to be true, I just couldn't believe it. I have been very transparent with our struggles of unbelief in this journey surrounding Abbey's testimony. This was one of those times. My religious thinking had such a dominant presence in my life that it was hard to process what we were hearing her share at times, even six months later.

A few days later I was on the phone with my dad's cousin, who lived in the same town in Georgia as we did. She knew all about Abbey's accident and her testimony. She loved every bit of Abbey's story and fiercely defended it. Every time my cousin would call she would ask me if Abbey had shared any more. On this particular day when she called and asked me, I hesitantly told her about what Abbey had said about meeting my grandmother. I explained to her how I just didn't think she was remembering correctly because she said my grandmother chased her around and tickled her and that seems so out of character for my grandmother.

My dad's cousin quickly interrupted me and said with a confidence in her voice, "That absolutely is just like Aunt Jean! She would come over to our house all the time and all of us kids would all run and hide because she would come chase us and tickle us. Aunt Jean had a way of pinning us to the floor and we couldn't get out of her grip and she would tickle us until we would scream, stop!" She continued to say that she was just the best and everyone's favorite Aunt. She said she believed every word Abbey said because she herself knew Aunt Jean to be that way with all the kids. My grandmother was my cousin's aunt, and her and her siblings grew up very close to my Grandparents.

This was a shock to me because although my grandmother loved us kids I just don't ever remember my Grandma running around tickling us. It just didn't seem like something she would do. I called my dad and shared with him what Abbey had said to get his perspective since it was his mom. I had not yet shared this story with my dad because I knew how close he was to his mom and I didn't want to share anything that may not have happened and cause his heart to hurt. Since my cousin had shared with me that it was very much like Grandma to do that I thought maybe it wouldn't hurt to get a second opinion from her oldest son. When I explained to my dad everything Abbey told me about my grandmother chasing her, tickling her, and laughing with her all I heard was silence on the other end followed by tears. He said, "That sounds like mom." He explained to me that in her later years of life, after the loss of her daughter Susie, she had changed and slowed down. When she lost her daughter to an accident with a broken heater she wasn't quite the same. She just didn't have the same pep in her step. He also explained that my grandmother had quite a few health challenges in her later years that prevented her from having all the energy she had back in her early thirties.

When I got off of the phone with my dad, I just sat there thinking about how wonderful it was to have Abbey meet her, my beautiful grandmother who I absolutely adored. She was the woman who discipled me growing up, and instilled a love for the Holy Spirit in me. The woman who would stay up all night praying for me even if all I had was a cold. As tears ran down my face I was amazed once again at how loving and good God is. The reason Abbey never said she met my grandmother is because my grandmother didn't introduce herself to Abbey; she just spent time with her. Abbey had no idea who she was, just that she was nice and played with her. I thanked the Lord once again for allowing her to meet her and theologically I just didn't even try to explain it. My grandmother knew the Lord, in fact she was a giant in the faith in my family's eyes. Two of her sisters even named one of their daughters after her and they told me it was in hopes that her anointing/mantle would be passed down to them. If scripture is true (and it is), and to be absent from the body is to be present with the Lord, then for a brief time both Abbey and my grandmother were in the same glorious place! How could I argue with that? Only unbelief in my heart would argue at this point. Abbey wasn't talking with the dead as some would say isn't allowed scripturally… she was dead.

12

The Faith of a Child ...

Eight months had gone by and she was still telling us little treasures about her journey to Heaven and her friendship with Jesus. I wish I could remember all of the stories. I wrote down as many as I could ... but there were so many. Sometimes weeks would go by before something would remind her of what she experienced. Sometimes it would be as simple as we would be driving and flowers on the side of the road would spark a memory.

I remember one day the girls were acting out a play they had written. They loved to put on plays for us. One day after school my older daughter, Elizabeth was lining her sisters up one by one in front of the French doors of our office. She was pretending that they were waiting to enter a store when Abbey suddenly said in an excited voice, "Hey this is what they have in heaven!" I quickly asked her before she would get distracted, "What do they have, doors?" She said with a big smile but a little confused on how to explain, "No, they have a big tall gate and it's white and pretty and people are standing lined up like this to get in. There are gates all over heaven, mama." I asked her if people were lined up all over Heaven and she said they weren't, just in front of the one gate and she didn't remember when exactly or how she saw it. I asked her if she was in that line and she said no she was with Jesus and that they were on the other side of the gate. She remembers it being really big, tall and white, while others were golden. She also reminded me of the walkways she walked on with Jesus, something she had told me when she first had her accident. Her description of the walkways, were little walkways that were curvy and golden and they were made with bricks. She said everywhere she would go she would see these little streets and gates. I loved her little child-like descriptions of heaven. It's something I will cherish for all my life. Our little talks and watching her sweet, little face light up whenever she would remember things she saw in Heaven will forever be imprinted in my heart and mind.

Abbey went back to playing and her sisters and I just stood there and looked at each other. Her sister's shrugged their shoulders and went on to continue acting out their play while I tried to take everything she had just shared in.

Whenever Abbey shares something new there is always a little bit of silence afterwards and this time was just the same. I didn't quite understand everything she had shared but I would remind myself this is from a little girl's perspective. I would remember to pause and allow myself to see things through the eyes of a child.... to let go of my understanding and my religious mindset. Let me clarify what I just said, to let go of my religious mindset. I didn't say to let go of what's scriptural.

Jesus said, *"Assuredly, I say to you, unless you are converted and become as little children, you will by no means enter the kingdom of heaven. Therefore whoever humbles himself as this little child is the greatest in the kingdom. Whoever receives one little child like this in My name receives Me." (Matthew 18 2-5)* Maybe this is why so many children have seen Heaven and have had visions and dreams of Jesus because their faith hasn't been tainted by the world. Maybe us adults should take more time to listen to children, we could learn a lot from their pure, untainted faith.

I never overlooked scripture and I didn't have to. I just have a tendency to understand God on an earthly level instead of looking at what she was saying through the lens of heaven. We live here on earth so our understanding of Heaven tends to be through our lens here on earth. When I read the book of Revelation I am blown away by the things I read. The throne room of God alone causes me to pause and think for a minute. Do we see living creatures here on earth full of eyes on the front and back of them? Do we see Seraphim flying with a piece of coal to cleanse our lips like Isaiah 6 talks about? No! Of course not but for some reason we can read these scriptures and know what we are reading is the truth but when a three year old is resurrected from her death and comes back saying she spent time in Heaven with Jesus we tend to doubt or criticize. We doubt even when what she is saying lines up with scripture.

I did immediately go searching the scriptures when she said this and I found in Revelation 21 where it talks about gates and specifically ones made of pearl. It refers to gates being in the New Jerusalem. I have to imagine that a lot of what will be in the New Jerusalem may emulate what is in Heaven now so it may not be far-fetched for her to have seen gates everywhere that were a pretty color of white. Perhaps, what she saw were gates made of pearls.

I knew that I didn't doubt her. What she experienced was special. It was a beautiful experience that was meant to be shared as a testimony to the goodness of God.

For far too many years and far too many times I struggled to write this story for my precious daughter. Fear has plagued my heart and mind more times than I can count. Fear of the criticism of man often would take over my confidence, and wreak havoc on my thoughts. I had to come to the realization that the only fear I should have in my heart is the fear of the Lord. I was allowing fear to take root in my life and lead me rather than allowing the Holy Spirit to lead me.

I prayed that Abbey would never lose her beautiful understanding of Him, and that her childlike faith would remain for all her life. Abbey's faith never changed after her accident, if anything it grew and only got stronger. In fact, all of our faith grew as a result of what happened on Sept 6th, 2014.

In a lot of ways Abbey's testimony paved the way for us to have our son, our baby who completed our family. Her testimony was the beginning of God's refining process in me to prepare me for so much more that He had for our family. Her testimony and journey to Heaven started a long wilderness season for me where the Lord ripped things out of me I didn't realize were there like unbelief and religious spirits. That season ended with trust and faith increased and a beautiful addition to our family named Liam. It was all necessary in order to move forward with His plan for our family. Now being on the other side of it I am so grateful to have gone through it.

One testimony to this increased faith and dependency on the Lord was in 2019. We were living in Colorado again and we were battling some health issues with our son. He was very sick his first year of life with various respiratory issues. He had many tests run on him and had seen over 34 doctors just in his first year of life. No one seemed to be able to figure out why he developed so many respiratory illnesses such as Pneumonia, RSV, etc. This was a constant battle we were at the time walking through.

We were out running errands with Abbey, Faith and Liam (our son) when Liam had an incident where he suddenly stopped breathing. I was in the car nursing him while Jason and our girls were in the store picking up probiotics for Liam. I noticed Liam struggling to breathe; he had not stopped breathing he was just struggling at this point. After trying to burp him and blowing in his face, nothing had changed. I grabbed my phone to try and dial 911 and my phone was not working there was no service, I tried but nothing was happening. I knew I had seconds to get him help so I ran into the store praying along the way that God would have Jason come out into the aisle as soon as I walked in. That is exactly what happened. I walked in and there was Jason with the girls at the end of the other end of the store. I screamed for him and said help! He dropped everything in his arms and they ran to me as fast as they could. Liam had not yet stopped breathing but was still struggling. This all took a matter of a minute or less. Believe it or not you can do a lot when you have adrenaline and God helping you. We jumped in our car and immediately drove across the street to an emergency room. Liam had stopped breathing and was flailing his arms in the air and was starting to turn blue but his heart never stopped beating. We knew he needed help and oxygen right away. Jason ran inside with Liam while I parked the car with the girls. I prayed out to the Lord, "Not again, not with another child, please God help us!" I was panicked and in a complete state of shock but also had a peace that instantly flooded my heart after praying.

When we entered the hospital this sweet, older man who worked there as a volunteer brought me and our younger two girls back immediately. I will never forget what happened next, something I will forever cherish in my heart. While I held my two little girls' hands, I could hear Faith praying under her breath with boldness, commanding life to take hold of Liam's body. On my other hand I watched Abbey just pray quietly as we walked back to where their little brother was. We entered the emergency room where several doctors and nurses were working on Liam. He looked so small laying on this big hospital bed in a room full of machines hooked up to him. Just as tears started to stream down my face, I watched Abbey's little hands lift in the air and she started to sing with a boldness I had never seen or heard come out of her, *"I raise a hallelujah, in the presence of my enemies, I raise a hallelujah, louder than the unbelief, I raise a hallelujah, my weapon is a melody, I raise a hallelujah, Heaven comes to fight for me."*

As she continued to sing over her little brother who was only around 8 months old at the time, I could see tears streaming down some of the nurses and doctors faces as they all listened to her. Instantly Liam started to breathe normally and his lungs opened up and his heart rate came down. No meds had been given to him yet when this happened in fact they were in the process of getting the meds ready. There was a shift in the atmosphere when Faith prayed and when Abbey sang over their brother. It was a team effort. Later, I asked Abbey why she did that and she told me she remembered recently hearing the story about why that song was written and she thought if it worked on the little boy the song was written about then it would work on Liam.

    I share that story to give a peek into our world after Abbey's accident. The effects it had on us was indescribable. The way it changed all four of my daughters' faith is hard to even sum up with words. My girls, who didn't experience what Abbey did, grew in their understanding of who Jesus was through her story. Did this have to happen to increase our faith? No, of course not, but God uses things the enemy meant to harm us with for good by turning it all around. We were already head over heels in love with Jesus before all of this happened; this just gave us even more of a reason to continue telling people about Him. A commission if you will, to tell people He is real and He loves them so extravagantly.

    I asked the girls if at any point they have felt less than or in the background because of Abbey's story. I was worried about each of them feeling like their testimony wasn't powerful in comparison to Abbey's testimony of going to heaven. Maybe it's a mom thing to worry about these things but I wanted to make sure they knew what they had to say was just as important and just as needed in this world. Faith answered me with so much wisdom, "No mama, this is her testimony to tell and I am just so thankful she can tell it." She explained how each of them has her own story to tell of what Jesus has done for them and she hoped she could help be a support for Abbey in any way she could just like she knows Abbey will support her. I loved that answer. As a mama you try to make sure everyone feels the same amount of love and attention. Each of our kids is so uniquely gifted and they each have a deep love for God. I have no doubt they will each do what God has called them to do and with great faith and grace.

13

Bye Bye, Abbey

I am going to close this book out with our favorite part of Abbey's journey to heaven, the part where she was sent back to us…

I have to rewind and go back to when her accident had just happened. It had only been a week or so and we were all eating dinner at the table one evening. Abbey said to me, "Mama, why was daddy holding me in the car and I wasn't in my car seat?" I stopped eating and answered her, "He had to hold you honey to try to get you to stay awake, you were having a hard time breathing and you kept wanting to go back to sleep." That was the best way to describe to my three year old what was happening to her while she was in our car. In reality she was unresponsive and her body was trying to shut down, she would stare right through us and every time she would stop breathing her eyes would start to roll back in her head. As I have said before, Jason would blow in her face and pinch her heels in an effort to cause her little body to take steady breaths and to stay alive.

I explained to her how it was safer to be in daddy's arms this one time than in her car seat. She seemed to understand what I was saying but then she said something that left us speechless. "Ok, well that's where the angels brought me back to daddy, it was in our car." At this point we all stopped eating and just paused for a minute. I asked her, "You mean they brought you back to our room on our bed?" She looked confused and replied, "No, they brought me back to the car in the front seat. Was I in your room?" I looked at her and explained how she was for a little bit. She had no recollection of any of that and it seemed to be confusing her. I didn't continue explaining the events that happened when her daddy had to perform CPR on her in our room.

It was after this conversation with Abbey where I had realized what I had felt in my heart to be true was in fact confirmed. I knew in my heart Abbey hadn't returned to us until we were in the car on the way to the hospital. I wrestled with this because her heart began to beat again on our bed but her spirit and her life just weren't there. Jason knew this as well and so did our girls. It's what caused us to desperately pray and storm Heaven on the way to the hospital. We wanted to see her sparkly green eyes see us again, not just stare through us.

She has zero recollection of ever even being in our room and had no clue her daddy had carried her to our car. She only remembered two angels who she described as large men, bigger than her Papaw, carrying her from our garage floor to Heaven and then carrying her back to our car in the front seat where we were praying fervently for her as a family.

I was reminded of the scripture in Luke 16:22 when the beggar died and was carried by angels. It seems like foolishness to our natural mind or I should say to our unsaved natural mind but just as the Bible says in *1 Corinthians 2:14, "But the natural man does not receive the things of the Spirit of God, for they are foolishness to him."* When we receive Christ those things which we thought to be foolish, the spiritual things, are no longer foolish. We are given a measure of discernment and faith and we walk by that from that point on. Angels taking us away seems crazy but then it doesn't when we live for a world we cannot see.

Abbey continued sharing her story about the angels bringing her back while we all sat at the table and listened. I asked her, "Abbey, did Jesus go with the angels to bring you back to us?" She answered, "No mama He called the same angels who brought me to Heaven over to Him, and Jesus said to them I need you to take her back to her mommy and daddy."

She explained to us how before Jesus asked the angels to take her back to us He kneeled down and said something to her. I asked her what He told her and what she responded with were the words that gave Abbey her assignment. They were my favorite words Jesus spoke to her while she was in His care. She said Jesus looked at her and He said, "Abbey, I need you to go back to your mommy and daddy now and I need you to do something for me. I need you to tell the whole world I AM REAL and I am coming back soon! Can you do that for me?" Abbey said yes to what Jesus asked her to do and then Jesus gave her a great big hug, a kiss on her cheek and then said three little words to her. These three little words are words I am forever grateful for. They were words that were more for me, her daddy, and those who love her than probably for her. He said to her, "Bye, bye Abbey."

As we sat there eating dinner listening to her tell us the end to her time in heaven, my heart was filled with thankfulness. I had tears streaming down my face while Abbey shared with us her final moments with Jesus. I put my hand over my mouth and gasped. I realized something right then; had Jesus not spoken those three powerful words to her, "Bye bye, Abbey," I wouldn't have my little girl with me now. I left the table and put my plate away and went upstairs to my room where I just sobbed and sobbed. I remember telling Jesus that there was no amount of words to pray that would adequately show my thankfulness to Him for telling my Abigail Joy goodbye. His goodbye meant our reuniting with her. I was so broken and humbled that He would allow us to have her back. I knew she wasn't ours to keep forever and that she belonged to the

Lord. I knew she had an assignment from Jesus that He gave her himself. And I promised that we would do our best to help her fulfill her yes to Jesus' request.

I also realized that what Jesus told Abbey to do for Him sounded an awful lot like what He told His disciples and all who follow Him in Matthew 28. He gave the Great commission before He left them to go to the Father. Before He said goodbye to Abbey He commissioned her as well.

One thing that stood out to me was the kiss Jesus gave her on her cheek. At first I thought how sweet it was that He kissed her on her cheek but then I started thinking about that a little more. I knew a kiss on the cheek in Jewish culture meant so much more than what it does in our Western culture. In Jewish culture it was a greeting men and women would give one another when they said hello or goodbye. A kiss on the cheek was a sign of great respect and honor and deep love for one another. When Judas kissed Jesus on the cheek as a sign that Jesus was the One they were to arrest, it was even more hurtful to Jesus than just the betrayal itself. Judas knew what a greeting with a kiss meant yet he still decided to betray him with it. Judas was basically stating with his kiss, this man that I honor and respect and love deeply, I am handing him over to you.

Jesus' kiss to Abbey in the same manner meant so much more to me than just a "Goodbye Abbey." It was a sign to me that he loved my little girl deeply, and He respected and honored her life. What a beautiful King we serve who loves us more than we could ever possibly imagine.

That night I hugged her so tight. I didn't want to let her go. I didn't know exactly how to process what I felt but I just knew whatever Jesus wanted us to do with her story we would. Whatever assignment He gave her we would make sure it was completed.

The next day in my devotion time I was thinking about how Abbey had told me that Jesus called her Abbey and not Abigail. I remember having many conversations with her before her accident about her name. We named her Abigail Joy and she had recently wanted to be called Abbey. I would tell her that her name was

Abigail not Abbey and that Abbey was just a nickname. She would just laugh with me and say, "No mama, my name is Abbey." When I asked her what Jesus called her she just smiled her great big Abbey smile. To see Abbey when she smiles, is to see a little girl whose smile swallows up her entire face. She said while giggling, "Jesus called me Abbey!" She covered her little mouth with her hand and just laughed and laughed knowing our many conversations about this. I smiled and said, "Well He knows you well then."

I thought about how when we hear our name being called out it brings comfort and a sense of belonging to something or someone. Scripture tells us in *Isaiah 43:1-2* *"But now thus says the Lord, who created you, O Jacob, And he who formed you, O Israel: Fear not, for I have redeemed you; I have called you by your name; You are mine."* This is as true today as it was then. Names are a big deal to God; they are so meaningful to Him and us.

He loved her so much that He even paid attention to the very details of what makes Abigail happy. From Jesus calling her the name she loved to her love of twirling round and round. He showed her the beauty of Heaven and introduced her to so many different people.. He allowed my grandmother to spend some time with her and He showed Abbey the river and tree of life. He showed her his scars and taught her things she didn't know. But most of all He spent time with her and provided comfort for her which is the best part of her journey to heaven. He took such good care of my baby when I couldn't. When we were doing everything we could to get her back to us He was dancing with her and taking her on walks and showing the beautiful things in heaven. What an amazing God we serve, He pays attention to the details of our lives.

Do I still call her Abigail? Yes I do, it's an argument I wasn't willing to give in to but we also call her Abbey quite often and she has grown to love both of her names.

Our story ended differently than most when she was given back to us. Some may ask why us? Why did we get a happy ending? I understand on so many levels that so many families don't get a second chance. We were overjoyed and thankful for our Abbey being sent back to us but there is also a deep ache inside for those who didn't get our ending. I almost didn't write this book or do any interviews in fear that there would be those who felt like God didn't hear their cry or that He somehow loved us more. He doesn't. He is no respecter of persons and He loves you just the same as He loves us.

I understand what it means to lose a loved one and the ache it leaves behind. I have not escaped the pain of death. I tragically lost my brother when I was just twelve years old and I personally know the effects that death has on a family. I would never want any family to experience the same grief we went through. It's something no one can possibly understand unless they have walked through it. Whenever I hear of someone who has lost a loved one I cringe on the inside because I know the anguish they are experiencing. I also know that if they will lean into the Father He will walk them through it and He will heal and restore something only He can do.

I know what it's like to weep with those who weep and rejoice with those who rejoice like scripture tells us to do in Romans. I believe when we learn how to do this.…weep with others and rejoice with others it teaches us true compassion, it strips all remnants of jealousy and envy from our hearts and it allows God to rightly place us in situations where He can trust us.

I have a special compassion for families affected by loss. I pray that Abbey's story brings *hope* to the hearts of those who encounter Abbey's testimony, not comparison or jealousy. That is one of the purposes of sharing her story. God commissioned her to tell the world that He is real and that He is coming back soon, we are just vessels to help her fulfill such a commission.

Abbey still talks about Heaven and Jesus to this day. She is still in awe of His love for her and she still tells her story as often as she can and when the Lord makes a way for her to.

Two years after Abbey's accident; when Abbey had an incident with her friends, who accused her of making it all up, we decided to put the idea of writing a book about Abbey's experience on the shelf. We originally had only planned on doing it to be able to have a record for her and our family of what happened and what she experienced. Having those few come against her had really taken the wind out of our sails at the time and caused us to slow down even sharing the story as much. I am a mama bear and I couldn't stomach the thought of any others accusing my baby girl of making it all up. It devastated her and I just couldn't stand to see that look on her face again, not when she was this young. We also were very protective of her testimony and we didn't want anyone or anything to taint it.

I remember praying and asking the Lord to speak to Abbey when the season to tell her story was here, and until then it would go on the bookshelf. Abbey never stopped sharing her story but as far as what we would do with it, we waited on the Lord to tell Abbey when the season was here. I never mentioned anything to Abbey about what I had prayed.

It's amazing to me how so many can be touched by the testimony of Abbey, but one or two come against it, and in our hearts and minds it was enough to silence us…for a little while anyways. This was something else the Lord matured in me during my wilderness season, or I should say He pulled out of me…the fear of man's opinion. Looking back, their criticisms helped me greatly. I don't hold any grudges towards these few that came against Abbey and said hurtful things. In fact their words helped me overcome this major stronghold in my life. The fear of man was very evident in my heart and it needed to go.

In March of 2021, six years after her accident, Abbey came to me one afternoon and said, "Mama, I was praying and God spoke to me and said it's time to tell your story, Abbey." I stopped what I was doing and turned to her and said, "Wow, really?" I was a little hesitant because of the timing of it all. We had just started a church and with five kids and homeschooling we were busy to say the least. Abbey insisted she heard from the Lord and my response to her was simple, "Ok honey well let's see how we can start making that happen." I honestly didn't know how that was going to work out, I am not a writer and the two in our household who are gifted with writing were so unbelievably busy at the time. I told Abbey "if the Lord told you its time, and I believe He did, then He will direct our next steps and make a way."

About two weeks later I received a phone call out of the blue from an old friend wanting to interview me about one of the testimonies we had as a family. She knew of several times when the Lord had intervened on our behalf and she wanted me to share one of those testimonies.

Assuming she wanted me to share Abbey's story I shared it on her program. To my surprise she had not even heard about what happened with Abbey. A week after I shared Abbey's story on my friend's show we received another phone call asking us to share Abbey's story on another ministry's show. After that we received so many emails that spoke of encouragement and healing after loss that we knew it was time to write this book.

I also knew that there was no possible way I could come close to telling all that Abbey saw and experienced in a single sit-down style interview. There was too much to share and to write it in a book would give people the details they were looking for.

The beautiful side to sharing Abbey's story was the many testimonies we received. My biggest fear when I did the interviews was not what man would say about us or my precious Abbey and her story. As I have said before, a big fear of mine was her story hurting mamas and daddies out there that had lost their babies. I just couldn't bear the thought of anyone feeling or thinking God loved us more or that He forgot about them. Because that just isn't the God I serve. The God I serve saw my family through the death of my brother and He was there to pick up the pieces of my shattered life. He was also the same God who healed and resurrected my daughter Abbey. No matter what valley you find yourself in, God is good. He always has been and He always will be the answer. He is the answer whether it's to the grieving heart or the heart crying out for healing. He is always good in every season of life.

What happened when I told her story publicly was the opposite of what I expected. We received so many beautiful emails and testimonies about mamas and daddies receiving healing when listening to Abbey's testimony. Healing from the loss of their own children. Testimonies about how much comfort they felt when reading about how Jesus took such good care of Abbey while she was in Heaven and how they knew He was doing the same for their loved ones.

When I read every single one of these emails and comments I wept for hours. I was so humbled and incredibly thankful that so many found peace and comfort. This is exactly what our prayer was and is for Abbey's story - that it be a testimony to the love, power, and healing nature of Jesus.

Her memory of what she saw in Heaven stopped at around a year after her accident, meaning she didn't remember much more after that. A few days ago she randomly remembered something she had never told me and I kept that for us. It was something we decided we won't share with the world. We shared what she felt we were supposed to share and the rest we kept for us to hold onto.

We prayed over this book and we cried many tears writing it. We went through a tremendous amount of warfare in writing it as well, so I know God's plans for this testimony is to bring freedom and healing to so many hearts that are heavy and broken.

I pray that every single person who reads this would feel God's love and the power of His Holy Spirit. That every soul would know Jesus is real, that you would place your trust in Him as your Lord and Savior and be assured of the promise that He is coming soon! I pray your faith is lifted and that you are more in love with Jesus than before when you started reading this. I pray that if you have experienced grief and are walking around with a broken heart that you would take comfort in the One who holds the keys to death, hell, and the grave. That you would know He longs to exchange your ashes for beauty and to pour His oil of joy over you for your mourning. I pray that you would be assured in your heart that God is still a healer; whether it is a broken heart or a broken body, Jesus bore stripes and endured suffering to heal us today! Heaven is a wonderful place that God has prepared for those who love Him but it's Jesus who made Heaven amazing for Abbey. I pray Jesus is who you see all throughout her testimony. He is good and He is the answer to every need we may have.

We hope that Abbey's testimony and her journey to Heaven and back, and her meeting Jesus, brings a sense of hope and peace. Most importantly we pray that her story will bring you into a saving knowledge and relationship with Jesus Christ, Abbey's friend and Savior.

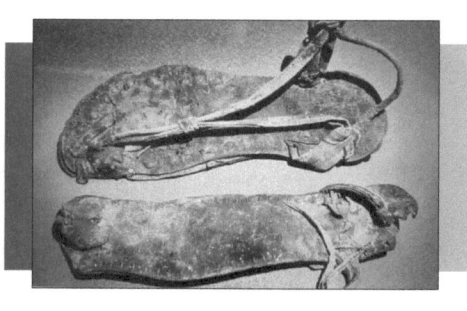

These are the sandals that were excavated and believed to be from when Jesus walked the earth. They are on display alongside the Dead Sea Scrolls in the Israel Museum in Jerusalem.

These are a modern rendition of what the excavated sandals would have looked like when Jesus walked the earth.

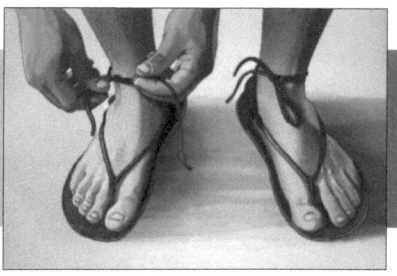

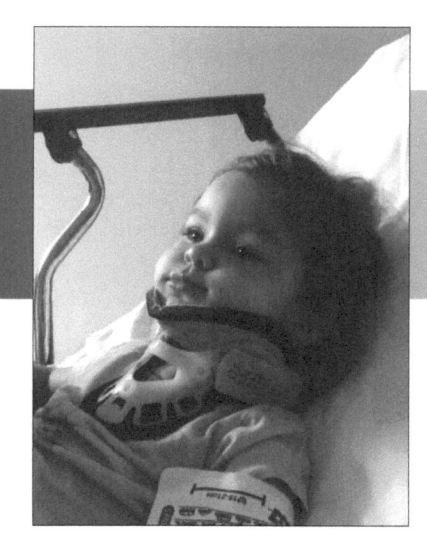

Abbey on her way to Children's Hospital before the bleeding on her brain was healed.

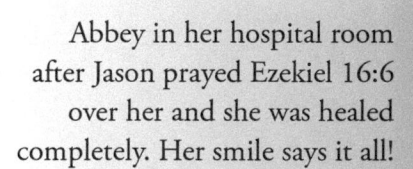

Abbey in her hospital room after Jason prayed Ezekiel 16:6 over her and she was healed completely. Her smile says it all!

About the Author

Sarah Boone is a wife, mother of five children and Bible College graduate with a degree in Practical Ministry. Born and raised in San Diego, CA, Sarah now resides in Northern Colorado with her husband Jason where they have planted and pastor a church and are contending for revival (www.revivalhouse.co). Sarah has spent the last twenty years pouring into and discipling women young and old. Her passion is to see people healed and restored by encountering the power of the Holy Spirit and coming to the saving knowledge of Jesus Christ.

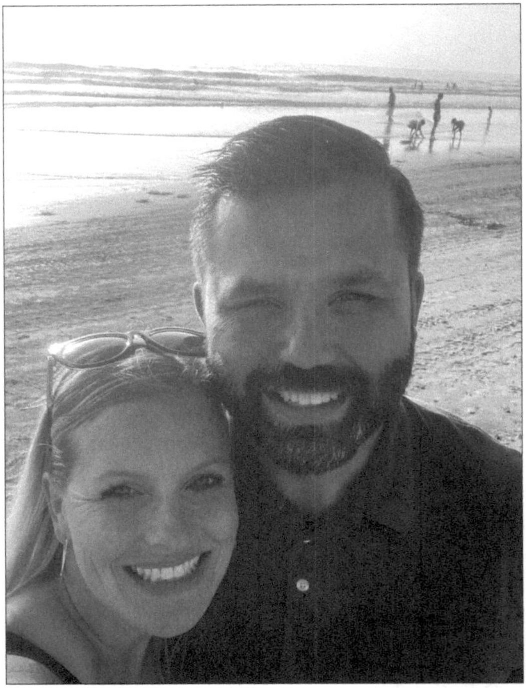

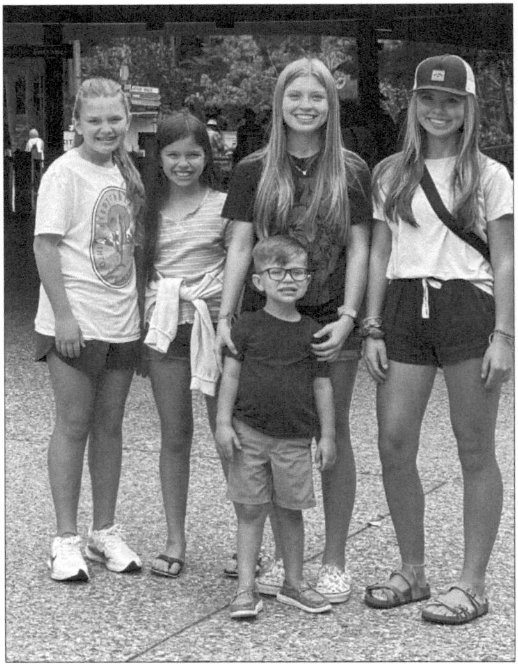

Made in United States
Troutdale, OR
04/04/2025